Your First Financial Steps

Your First Financial Steps

Nancy Dunnan

HarperPerennial

A Division of HarperCollins*Publishers*

HarperCollins books may be purchased for educational, business, or sales promotional use. For information, please write: Special Markets Department, HarperCollins Publishers, Inc., 10 East 53rd Street, New York, NY 10022.

FIRST EDITION

Library of Congress Cataloging-in-Publication Data
Dunnan, Nancy.
    Your first financial steps / by Nancy Dunnan.—1st HarperPerennial ed.
        p.   cm.
    ISBN 0-06-273251-X
    1. Finance, Personal—United States.   I. Title.
HG179.D864   1994
332.024—dc20   93-31860

95 96 97 98 99 PS/RRD 10 9 8 7 6 5 4 3 2 1

Contents

To Anne Rockwell Rapp and the twenty-to-thirty-something Packs: Loren, Jeffrey, Ellen, and Barbara.

Special thanks to the following people for their help and expertise:
Marcy Ross, Researcher
Tom Heller, Taxes
Barbara Pack, Healthcare
Robert Klinek, Real estate

And to Robert Wilson and Eric Newman for their editorial work.

Introduction

Getting Your Financial Act Together

When you graduated you probably thought classes were over—yet there's one course left, and one that's not taught in school—Personal Money Management 101.

A wonderful sense of freedom and independence accompanies being on your own, cashing a paycheck, being able to take care of yourself, surviving without your parents' money.

Yet you could botch it. You could make a major or minor mess out of it. You could run up credit card bills and find yourself heavily in debt, with no money left over for extras—for the fun things in life like a vacation, car or a night out with friends. You could figure that because you're young and healthy you don't need medical insurance. You could figure that the person you live or room with will always pay his or her portion of the rent on time. You could figure you're job is secure so you don't need a huge savings account. You could figure that there will always be someone to bail you out.

You could be wrong. That's what this book is all about—how not to botch it, how to fix it up if you have botched it, and how to easily and intelligently handle your income so that you not only take care of yourself but also establish sound financial moves now, while you're still twenty or thirty something, that will carry you through the rest of your life.

Getting your financial act together is not very difficult, especially if you realize that much of what we do in life is based on habit. You put your left sock on first. You drink your coffee with milk. You jog before work. You listen to the evening news. You always have popcorn at the movies. You recycle your newspapers and bottles. So too it is when dealing with money. How you spend, save and invest are all habits. It's just as easy to develop smart money habits, and as with eating healthy, to benefit from the long-term payoff.

This book is divided into five sections. There's no need to read it from cover to cover unless you want to—you can dip in and out of various chapters as they have relevance in your life,—with two exceptions. Required reading: pages 187 to 208 in the "House-keeping" chapter which cover simple, painless ways to set up a budget and save on a regular basis, and the following section, "Keeping It Together: A Seven-Step Course."

Keeping It Together:
A Seven-Step Course

If you're the type who burns the candle at both ends and never has a bad hair day, you can take one financial step per day and have your financial house in order by the end of the seventh day. If, however, you're like the rest of us, implement one step a month so that around the middle of the year everything will be in place.

STEP ONE: DEFINE YOUR FINANCIAL GOALS
STEP TWO: GET ORGANIZED
STEP THREE: EDUCATE YOURSELF
STEP FOUR: MAKE A BUDGET
STEP FIVE: SAVE SOME & INVEST SOME
STEP SIX: KNOW WHERE YOUR MONEY IS
STEP SEVEN: TREAT YOURSELF

Step One: Define Your Financial Goals

Like the corporation or business you work for (or own), a game plan and set of goals make for a smooth running operation and continual accountability. So, too, it is with your own life. And in fact, the first step toward being financially savvy is to have a plan, one based on personal goals. These goals are your very own and there's no reason why they have to be like your best friend's, your sister's or your parents'. Even if you are living with someone or are married, you should draw up both individual and joint goals.

To keep these goals uppermost in your mind, take time to write them down. Just as with the CEO of a corporation, you'll find it helpful to list both short-term goals (those that can be accomplished in a year or less) and long-term goals (those that take longer to achieve). Then, assign a due date to each one and using the accompanying worksheet, determine how much you need to save to reach each goal.

Some examples to get you started:

- To find an apartment
- To paint and decorate
- To buy a car
- To go back to school
- To take a vacation
- To visit an old school friend
- To pay back a loan
- To get rid of credit card debt
- To invest in my company's savings/retirement plan
- To buy a house

Photocopy this worksheet and fill it in.

Meeting My Goals

Goal	Amount Needed	Target Date	Saving Periods	$ Saved per Period
Vacation	$850	July 1	25 weeks	$34

Step Two: Get Organized

Chaos and lost papers wreak havoc with meeting goals—whether at work or at home. So, set aside a Saturday morning to get your financial house in shape. Make individual files for:

- bank statements and canceled checks
- brokerage firm statements
- credit card statements
- warranties
- insurance policies
- bills (paid and to-be paid)
- retirement records
- automobile registration and insurance
- health care material
- receipts for major purchases
- tax-related papers

If this type of nitty-gritty detail blows you away, order *The Standard Homefile* which includes plastic-coated file dividers and a 48-page handbook; $19.95 plus $3.50 shipping, from: Financial Advantage, 800-695-3453; and 410-362-3766 in Baltimore, Maryland.

Step Three: Educate Yourself

Just as you had to learn skills and information in order to do your job, so too it is with a financial fitness program. You'll learn much of what you need in this book and there are plenty of other good sources—check your community college, local Y and school for adult education courses in personal finance. Subscribe to a financial publication . . . and read it. Two of my favorites are *Bottom Line Personal* (800-274-5611) and *Your Money* (800-777-0025). The business section of the newspaper is also very educational. Make it a point to listen to or watch the financial news every morning or evening. And, take notes: jot down the names of stocks that are discussed; information about the movement of interest rates, unemployment figures and other economic indicators; unfamiliar words. You'll soon find yourself feeling very much at ease with Wall Street concepts.

Step Four: Make a Budget

The only way to set up a safety net and also find money to invest is to save regularly. And the only way to save regularly is to spend less than you earn. Although putting out less than you take in is essentially a habit, it helps to have a budget, not only to get into the savings habit but also to stick to it. Keep a monthly journal, tracing your spending habits and when you are tempted to overextend, look back at your goals. It's much easier to skip an expensive night on the town when you know it puts off that trip to Europe.

Step Five: Save Some & Invest Some

Contrary to popular opinion, saving and investing are not precisely the same. Saving is a conservative, safe way to put aside money, one in which you know how much of a return you're receiving at any time—whether it's on a bank savings account or CD. With savings, both principal and interest are not at risk, whereas with investing neither is guaranteed. Yet many stocks, bonds, mutual funds, real estate, even collectibles can reap far greater rewards than pure savings. You need both savings and investments to round out your portfolio. For savings suggestions, read Chapter 7, "Simple Speedy Solutions for Small Savers." If you are a beginning investor, these four tips will get you started:

- Buy stock in the company you work for.
- Buy stock in your local utility company, if it's well run. Call the company's headquarters and ask the Investor Relations Department if you can buy shares directly from the company and avoid a brokerage commission. If not, use a discount stock broker.
- Buy stock in a company whose product or service you know and like.
- Reinvest any dividends you receive in additional shares of the stock. (Many corporations have automatic dividend reinvestment plans, known as DRIPs. Again, check with the Investor Relations Department.)
- Join or start an investment club and learn about the stock market with friends. For information, call the National Association of Investors Corp., 810-583-6242.

Step Six: Know Where Your Money Is

Like a business, once a year you need to take inventory and determine what you're worth—officially known as your net worth. It's the best way to track your financial progress over the years. Your net worth is simply your assets minus your liabilities and it lets you know how you're converting income into assets.

Finding Your Net Worth

Assets		Liabilities	
Cash on hand	$_____	Unpaid bills	$_____
Cash in checking account	$_____	Unpaid charge accounts	$_____
Savings account	$_____	Rent/mortgage	$_____
Money market fund	$_____	Income taxes	$_____
Certificates of deposit	$_____	Property taxes	$_____
Savings bonds	$_____	Loans (auto) (current value)	$_____
Cash value life insurance	$_____	Loan (educational)	$_____
Stocks, bonds (market value)	$_____	Loans (personal)	$_____
Pension (cash value)	$_____	Insurance premiums	$_____
House (market value)	$_____	Other	$_____
Furnishings	$_____		
Equipment (computer, etc.)	$_____		
Auto, bike, cycle	$_____		
Jewelry, antiques	$_____		
Collections (stamps, etc.)	$_____		
Value of business	$_____		
Other	$_____		
Total Assets:	$_____	Total Liabilities:	$_____

Now, subtract total liabilities from total assets:

Total Assets: $_____ Less Total Liabilities: $_____ =

TOTAL NET WORTH: $_____

Net worth is not difficult to calculate; simply use the worksheet on the previous page.

Then, make a list of expenses that were a waste or unnecessary. Once you've accomplished this task you'll quickly be able to pinpoint where to make changes. And, you may be very surprised at how much you are worth when you take into consideration cash on hand, your car, furniture, other possessions and any savings bonds, stocks or other investments you either received as gifts or purchased on your own.

Step Seven: Treat Yourself

Have fun with some of the money you've saved. You don't have to put aside everything for a rainy day or for your retirement. If you do, you'll be very dull company, indeed. Instead, at least once a year tap some of your savings and fulfill a dream: see a play, hire a decorator, spend a day at a fitness center, take scuba lessons, go dancing, buy a motorcycle, spend a night in a hotel, sign up for tennis camp, collect something you love, treat a friend to dinner, get a Christophe haircut, buy your own airplane on which to get your hair cut.

And, why not also take pleasure in helping someone else? Make a tax deductible donation to your school's scholarship fund, your public library or your favorite charity.

PART ONE

Your Working Life

You may be so excited about starting your career that you overlook investigating some things almost as important as your salary—taxes, employee benefits, especially health insurance—and, even though it is a long way off, retirement plans. Now that you're on your own and no longer protected by your parents or by being a student, you need to handle these things yourself. Let's start with your paycheck and taxes. Then we'll discuss how to take advantage of your company's fringe benefits or arrange your own.

"Work is more fun than fun."

Noel Coward

1 *Your First Job*

This chapter covers all those "firsts" related to working—including doing well in your new position, deciphering your company's benefits package and perks, understanding your paycheck, getting the right health insurance and even how to file your first income tax return—or at least make a stab at it.

Of course, it's a good idea not to be fired from your first job (or from any job, for that matter), so we'll begin with some hints for how to keep your paycheck coming in and then wind up this chapter with what to do if the ax should fall and you become "job-free."

> "By working faithfully eight hours a day, you may eventually get to be boss and work twelve hours a day."
>
> *Robert Frost*

Doing Your Job Well in Order to Keep It

Your best interview suit is wrinkled and your resume is suddenly out-of-date, and happily so, because you've landed a real job. You may be nervous, especially during those initial weeks or until that first evaluation. In the meantime, it's great to have a regular paycheck. Obviously, in order to keep it you must work hard and do your job well. Yet there are more subtle steps you can take to safeguard your job—even with cutbacks and layoffs in the wings. Management/bosses of major corporations prefer employees who:

- are punctual and don't make excuses
- when necessary will come in early or stay late
- put the company's interests first
- are thoughtful and enthusiastic but not ridiculously gung-ho
- keep their promises
- will admit it if they don't know something and then find out
- don't gossip on the job
- give credit to others when it's deserved
- are mannerly—polite to everyone, in person and on the telephone
- are honest
- don't take company supplies home (now that you're working you ought to be able to afford your own stamps, stationery, and telephone calls)
- speak well (remember, the older generation didn't grow up using four-letter words in their everyday conversation. Neither should you, even if everyone else does)

Making Yourself Too Valuable to Be Let Go
Not many years ago, if you landed a position in one of the nation's top companies, you were practically guaranteed a long-term job with benefits, regular raises and a good retirement plan. That's no longer true. No job in America is safe these days. In fact, the average job tenure in corporate America has declined by nearly

50% in the past decade, from 12.5 years in the mid-1980s to less than 7 today. To protect your position:

- *Know* your company's business, its history, strengths and weaknesses. Read whatever you can about its competitors as well.
- *Become known* within the company. That doesn't mean playing up to the boss, but it does mean making certain your talents are acknowledged. Volunteer for in-house committees (even if it's running your office's blood drive or baseball team), and join professional groups or your union.
- *Seize* leadership opportunities. Take various assignments when offered—you'll discover new strengths and become better known.
- *Be flexible.* Accept travel assignments, different hours or, if you can, relocate.
- *Re-tool.* Go back to school. Bring your skills up to speed. Know how to use computer software programs, new marketing techniques, advanced equipment, foreign markets. Many schools offer one- to four-week courses. Your employer may even pick up the tab. Go for it.

Upgrading Your Skills
The American Management Association offers nearly 3,000 seminars on 240 subjects, including information systems, sales, management, finance, public speaking at one- to four-day sessions in most major U.S. cities. Tuition is $100 to $2,000. Telephone: 518-891-1500.

- *Speak and write well.* America's managers continually complain that younger workers do not know basic English, cannot cogently present their ideas, make far too many grammatical and spelling errors. Evaluate your own abilities objectively and, if necessary, take a seminar or course to help you become a better writer and public speaker.

Where to Learn the Art of Speaking

Dale Carnegie has 14-week courses where you must give a speech to classmates each week. Check your local phone directory.

Toastmasters International, Box 9052, Mission Viejo, CA 92690. Telephone: 714-858-8255. Teaches communication skills in thousands of local clubs; check your phone directory or write to the headquarters.

SkillPath, 800-873-7545 or 913-362-3900, has one-day seminars on grammar, word usage, business writing and other skills in many cities.

- *Notice* the skills of the people most recently hired or promoted by your firm—a good clue to what management is looking for.

Other shrewd job strategies to implement include getting assignments in *before* deadlines, taking work home, getting along with your boss, your boss's assistant and even your boss's boss (then if your boss leaves, you'll be recognized by his/her immediate supervisor). And network. Keep a file of people's names, addresses, phone numbers and their positions; add a note about where you met or what they do. Keep in touch by sending them clippings or other information of interest.

And finally,

- *Start looking.* The best time to begin a job search is while you still have a job.

If You're Let Go

Before The Ax Falls

Most layoffs don't simply happen. They're usually preceded by a steady flow of "bad news" signs— bosses gathered behind closed doors, unscheduled board meetings, outsiders brought in to "fix things up." Raises are frozen. If you see it coming, you should immediately upgrade your skills, update your resume, and upscale your savings.

Finding Bridge Money

The average job search is about six months, so you'll need enough cash on hand to cover expenses for at least that long. Begin by cutting back on spending. Aim to lower your general expenses and credit card usage by 10 to 20%. Then, set up a new budget. Limit dining out (perhaps to once a week) and new clothes, put vacations on hold, take on no new debt, put off buying a house; foster a new and improved attitude toward money so that the financial fallout of losing a job is not as bad as it might be.

Take care, however, to budget for fun in your life as well. Don't whittle away everything. Keep up your golf, tennis, or squash game—the exercise is good, and you may just meet someone who can help you find a new job.

If you have a mortgage, check to see if it has a forbearance agreement that lets you pay nothing or a portion of the mortgage for a set period of time. Put your severance pay, if you get any, in a money market fund so it will earn interest yet allow you to still tap into it when needed . . . this is bridge money to keep you afloat while you find another job.

If you need a little more cash, inventory your possessions and sell what you can live without. Those extra

Sources of Bridge Cash	
Savings account	$_____
Money market fund	$_____
CDs	$_____
Other investments	$_____
Part-time work	$_____
Items to sell	$_____
Severance pay	$_____
Cash value of life insurance	$_____
Freelance	$_____
Other	$_____

TV sets, sports equipment, stereo, walkman, and motorcycle can go. If you have space, take in a roommate, or earn extra money with part-time or freelance work.

It might be a good idea to make copies of samples of your work and keep them at home; if you're fired or laid off, you're not likely to have the opportunity to put together a portfolio.

When You Get the Pink Slip

After you've been told officially that you no longer have a job, you may have about two days during which you may be able to negotiate some benefits from your employer—that's about how long management may feel guilty or at least uncomfortable about firing you. So, move quickly.

> *Negotiating severance pay.* Although severance packages are generally reserved for longer-time employees, you may be able to get something. You certainly won't if you don't ask. The average is one week of salary for every year of service, with a two- to three-month minimum. Other

components of severance may include salary continuation and pay for accrued vacation days.

Collecting pension payouts. You may find that you're being fired within months of being vested. Anyone within a year of vesting can challenge this decision in court—your employer knows this, so if you're close to your vesting date, ask that your pension be vested.

If you receive a pension payout, it may very well be the single largest sum of money you've ever received. It will be tempting to spend it, especially since it's a long way until retirement and you may be short of cash. But don't.

Have the money rolled over directly into an IRA. If you take the payout as cash, you will have to pay income tax plus a 10% premature withdrawal penalty. Adding insult to injury, Congress in 1993 started requiring employers to withhold 20% of any lump sum distributions made directly to the employee. In other words, if you get the check, you'll get only 80% of it. Have the payment rolled over into an IRA and not issued directly to you.

Keeping your health insurance. The Consolidated Omnibus Budget Reconciliation Act of 1985 (COBRA) allows you to continue with your company's health plan for up to 18 months. However, you have only 60 days in which to choose this option and put it into place. Your employer can charge you the full cost of the insurance premiums and an administrative fee—which will be a lot more than what you paid while you were working but less than buying your own coverage. Companies with fewer than 20 employees may offer benefits if they wish, but they're not obligated to do so.

If the termination date for your health insurance is near the end of the month, ask for the date to be shifted to the next month to get another month of health benefits.

Maintaining life insurance. If you have life insurance and dependents, you will want to maintain coverage while out of work. If your company does not continue this insurance, you may be able to convert the employer's group policy to an individual one. If your policy has accumulated cash, you can take this in a lump sum and use some of it to buy term coverage and save the rest. Or, you can borrow against the policy's cash value and pay it back when you're working again. You can also choose to have any dividends the policy pays go toward future premiums, thus cutting the cost of keeping your coverage intact.

Collecting Unemployment Compensation

After collecting your thoughts and taking a day or two of rest, and telling your family and friends about your new job-free status, you should begin your job search; but first, sign up for unemployment insurance. Many people who are fired fail to apply, apparently thinking they're not eligible or because they're embarrassed. That's a big mistake; this is a valuable source of cash, and one to which you are fully entitled. It may just keep you afloat until you land a new position.

Your unemployment office will be listed in the government services section of the phone book, under State Department of Labor or Unemployment Services. Call and ask what you need to bring in when you apply. Prepare to wait on long lines (bring a book). It takes a few weeks before you get a check.

Although each state sets its own benefit amounts and requirements for eligibility, all of them insist on proof that you have worked for a certain number of weeks during the past year—often 14 to 30 weeks. Most also require people to actively look for a new job, providing the names of their job contacts on a weekly basis.

Under rare circumstances unemployment insurance can be denied: if your employer can establish that you were fired for "just cause" or misconduct. Incompetence, missing work, or showing up late now and then is not regarded as misconduct, but fighting with a supervisor, chronic lateness, or stealing are.

If you quit work, you are usually ineligible for unemployment compensation, but you may be able to collect, depending upon why you quit. Reasons that usually count: sexual harassment, unsafe working conditions, or if the employer failed to pay overtime wages.

 Some employers encourage their employees to resign instead of being fired, hinting that resignation looks better on your resume. If you resign under such circumstances, you probably will not be eligible to collect unemployment compensation.

Your Paycheck and Taxes

Paycheck Stubs

If you work full time for a company, you'll notice when you get your paycheck that it's not anywhere near your full salary. That's because money is being withheld or deducted by your employer for federal, state, and local income taxes. Your paycheck stub itemizes what's been withheld for these taxes as well as for FICA—Social Security. In addition to tax withholdings, deductions for health insurance, union dues, and contributions to a 401(k) plan may be taken out.

> **FICA**
> This line on your paycheck stub represents your Social Security retirement tax. It stands for Federal Insurance Contributions Act and also includes a Medicare tax that goes to support the program adopted in 1965 to provide hospitalization benefits for senior citizens. Congress can increase the rate you pay and the upper limit of taxable income. You and your employer each pay half the rate.

 Keep paycheck stubs and compare them with your W-2 form (explained below). The information should match exactly.

Withholding and the W-4 Form

Withholding, which began during World War II when the government needed a steady flow of cash, involves your employer taking money from your income as a prepayment of your tax liability for the year, so that by December 31st you will have paid all (or nearly all) of your income taxes. The amount withheld from each paycheck is based on how you fill out the IRS W-4 form, which is then filed with your employer who in turn reports this amount on yet another IRS form, a W-2. A copy of the W-2 is sent to you by January 31st of the following year. By law, the amount withheld must be at least what you paid last year, or 90% of what you owe this year. If you underwithhold, you could be penalized.

On the W-4 form list the number of "allowances" or exemptions you claim. (An exemption is basically a discount on your tax bill.) There is a worksheet to help you figure out the number to claim. The more allowances you claim, the less withheld and the greater your take-home pay; however, there are specific rules regarding how many allowances or exemptions you can claim. If you are unmarried, for example, you can take one exemption. If you are married, or have children or other dependents, then you can claim more exemptions. Your company's personnel officer can explain the options.

IRS Publication 919, "Is My Withholding Correct?" has an easy-to-use worksheet. For a free copy, call 800-829-3676.

 Insist that the personnel officer go over the actual dollar amounts involved, using the withholding tables from the government, so you will know precisely how much will be withheld if you claim zero, one, two, or more allowances.

If you marry, have a child, divorce, or make changes in how you earn your income, update your W-4.

OVERWITHHOLDING TO GET A REFUND

Many people overwithhold, either as a way of enforced savings because they get a refund from the government or because they are skittish about being fined for underwithholding. Although there's no penalty for overwithholding, you're really giving the government use of your money that comes right out of your paycheck.

 Instead of overwithholding, have the minimum withheld and the rest automatically deducted from your paycheck through payroll savings and deposited into a money market fund where it will earn interest.

IF YOU HAVE SEVERAL JOBS

When you file your tax return, if you've had enough withheld from your paychecks, you won't have to pay any more to the government. However, if you are working more than one job, it's up to you to make certain enough is being withheld from all your paychecks; otherwise you may owe a whopping amount come April 15th, and unless you've been especially careful, you may have spent all that money.

The problem arises because each company you work for withholds as if that is the only money you will earn during the year—if you earn $15,000 in each of two part-time jobs, each employer will withhold less than if you had just one job earning $30,000. If you're in this position, consider taking zero exemptions rather than one on your W-4.

IF YOU ARE SELF-EMPLOYED

Freelancers, independent contractors, and other self-employed people do not have money withheld as the year goes along. So, if you fall into this category, you must pay estimated taxes, using a special IRS form, the 1040-ES, which has clear directions on how to calculate the amount due and send in payments. To get a copy, call the IRS at 800-829-3676. You can pay estimated taxes in one lump sum at the beginning of the year or in four quarterly amounts.

 Take care not to underpay—you must pay 90% of your total tax bill to avoid being penalized.

All About W-2 Forms

At the end of the year, actually before the end of January of the next year, you'll get a statement called a W-2 form from your employer showing your total salary for the year as well as how much was withheld in federal, state, and local taxes; in Social Security payments; and, if your state requires it, in state disability insurance. It also indicates whether you contributed to a deferred retirement plan such as a 401(k) or

403(b) plan, and notes certain benefits you may have received from your employer such as the use of a company car or reimbursements for child care expenses. If you worked in a restaurant, your tips are reported. If you worked in someone's house as a baby-sitter, housekeeper, cook, or in some other capacity, the amount you earned is given, provided you earned over $50 in any calendar quarter.

What About Babysitting?
If you babysit in your own home and determine "the nature and manner" of the services performed, you are considered to have self-employment income. But if you babysit in the parent's home and follow the parent's instructions, you are an employee of the parents and not self-employed.

When you file your income tax return (which you must do by April 15th unless you get an extension) you are required to include a copy of this form. But before filing, compare the W-2 figures against your paycheck stubs for accuracy, including that of your Social Security number. Report any errors to your employer.

Paying Your Taxes
"Nothing is more inevitable than death and taxes," observed Benjamin Franklin. Given the truth of his statement, we are all stuck paying the IRS.

Tax Highs and Lows
- The lowest income tax rate in the United States was 1% between 1913 and 1915.
- The highest rate was 91% in 1944.
- The highest rate in 1994 was 39.6%.

The first thing you need to know is that we have a progressive tax system in this country. That means the more you earn the higher the rate at which you pay. The second thing you need to understand is that how much you pay is determined by two factors: one's tax bracket and one's filing status.

- Tax brackets. Your income falls into a bracket or category. Each bracket has a set tax rate, and income is taxed at the rate for that bracket.

- Filing status. In addition to the tax bracket, your filing status also determines the amount of tax you pay. Taxpayers select one of five filing status choices: single, married filing jointly, married filing separately, head of household, and widow or widower with dependent child or children. Some of these categories pay more than others—for example, usually filing separately costs more than filing jointly, and filing as a single more than filing head of household. The IRS spells out who qualifies for what status in the directions on its forms and in its free publications.

How to Report Your Taxes

To file your taxes, you must complete one of three IRS forms: a 1040-EZ, a 1040-A, or a 1040. The form you use is determined by your filing status, how much money you earned during the year, how you earned it (from salary, wages, self-employment, dividend or interest, sale of assets), and the deductions or credits you take. Here's a quick rundown—you can get more info from IRS publication #17, "Your Federal Income Tax."

- *The 1040-EZ.* This, the simplest of the three forms, has only ten lines. To use it you must be single or married filing a joint return and earn less than $50,000 from salaries, wages, tips and interest income of less than $400.

- *The 1040-A.* Use this form if you do not itemize deductions and if you earn less than $50,000. You can be married, have income from several sources, and take the child care credit and/or IRA deduction and still file this form.
- *The 1040.* This more complex form, with some 60+ questions, is used by over half the nation's taxpayers. It also has some 70 additional forms and schedules that accompany it. You must use this if you itemize deductions.

Don't Forget to Pay Taxes on:

Back pay	Jury fees
Bonuses	Salary
Commissions	Severance pay
Director's fees	Sick pay
Dismissal pay	Tips
Employee prizes/awards	Vacation pay

If you filed taxes last year, the IRS knows where you are and will send you one of these forms in January. Or, you can get the forms at post offices, public libraries, regional IRS offices, or by calling the IRS at 800-829-3676. After completing the appropriate form, mail it along with a check for any amount you owe to the IRS processing center in your area. The address is on a preprinted envelope enclosed with the form. Or, call the IRS for the appropriate address. Your return must be postmarked by midnight of April 15th unless the 15th falls on a Saturday or Sunday, in which case you have until the next Monday.

If you cannot make the deadline, it's easy to get one

automatic extension—just send in Form 4868, "Application for Automatic Extension of Time to File U.S. Individual Income Tax Return," by April 15th. The IRS will give you until August 15th. If you're still behind the eight ball, additional extensions may be granted for certain reasons; use Form 2688. It's easy to make an error on a tax return—you may forget that you sold a stock, add figures incorrectly, or write in the wrong digit on your Social Security number. If that's the case, file Form 1040-X.

Itemized Deductions
Expenses such as mortgage interest, state and local taxes, charitable contributions, and medical deductions that are claimed on Schedule A of Form 1040 and which reduce your adjusted gross income and therefore your taxable income.

Your Tax Records
In order to file an accurate tax return, you need accurate records—those showing what you earned and, if you are itemizing deductions, proof of those expenses. Many records are sent to you automatically—by your employer, bank, mutual fund, companies that paid you dividends; they send duplicate copies to the IRS by January 31st. You are responsible for keeping track of earnings from rental income, freelance work, or royalties and reporting this income on your return. If you itemize deductions or claim the child care credit, you must provide the record of your expenses.

VERIFYING EXPENSES

Receipts, canceled checks, credit card slips with details recorded on the back, regular and detailed entries in an expense book or an appointment diary that include date, purpose of meeting, people involved—all these are acceptable to the IRS.

How Long to Keep Records

The general rule is that the IRS has three years in which it can audit your return, so keep all pertinent records at least that long. Longer is better because sometimes records or expenses overlap from one year to the next. In cases where income has not been reported, the IRS may go back as far as six years, and if it suspects fraud, there is no time limitation. Conservative accountants recommend keeping tax records forever.

Getting Help With Your Taxes

Unless you file a 1040-EZ, you may need some help in preparing your return. This may mean reading a tax guide, using a computer program, consulting an accountant, or asking your parents for assistance. But first, turn to the IRS—it's the cheapest source of information, with over 100 free publications, the most comprehensive of which is #17, "Your Federal Income Tax." The IRS also has a toll-free telephone service and a prerecorded information service, called Tele-Tax, that covers about 140 topics. Check your local phone directory for area numbers or call 800-829-4477. Many local libraries have IRS tapes and video cassettes with step-by-step directions on how to fill out forms and schedules.

If you have a slightly more complicated return—perhaps you are itemizing deductions, are self-employed, or have sizable nonsalaried income from a trust fund, consult a pro. You may need to do this only once and afterwards, until your life is more complicated or the tax code is changed, follow this example. Select someone who has had at least three or four years experience, preferably five or more; who does returns as a regular part of his or her business; and who has experience with your particular tax situation or needs. You will also want to know how much preparing the tax return will cost, and how much this person charges if you need advice during the rest of the year.

Don't Use a Tax Preparer Who

- Says no client was ever audited
- Has extremely low fees
- Guarantees you'll get a refund before even looking at your return
- Says the refund check will come to his office and be forwarded to you
- Refuses to sign his/her name on your tax return. Paid preparers are required by law to sign your return along with their address and ID number

---

Ways to Cut Taxes

The American cowboy and wit Will Rogers observed that "the income tax has made more liars out of the American people than golf has." I don't advocate lying about your taxes or your golf score, but you should take advantage of the few legitimate ways to reduce your tax bite. As you earn more money, have a family, or build a business you will be able to use these techniques and investments. And, you will also discover that tax planning well in advance of April 15th can save you money.

- Tax-free investments. The most common of these is municipal bonds, sold by state and local municipalities to raise money. The interest earned is free

Popular IRS Pamphlets
These free publications will help you with preparing your tax return, taking deductions, and getting tax credits. To order call 800-829-3676.

Number	Title
1	Your Rights as a Taxpayer
17	Your Federal Income Tax
463	Travel, Entertainment, and Gift Expenses
501	Exemptions, Standard Deduction, and Filing Information
502	Medical and Dental Expenses
503	Child and Dependent Care Expenses
504	Divorced or Separated Individuals
505	Tax Withholding and Estimated Tax
508	Educational Expenses
520	Scholarships and Fellowships
525	Taxable and Nontaxable Income
526	Charitable Contributions
529	Miscellaneous Deductions
531	Reporting Income from Tips
533	Self-Employment Tax
550	Investment Income and Expenses
552	Recordkeeping for Individuals
587	Business Use of Your Home
910	Guide to Free Tax Services
919	Is My Withholding Correct?
926	Employment Taxes for Household Employers

from federal income tax, and if you live in the state or city where bonds are issued, free from state and/or local income taxes.

> "I'm proud to be paying taxes in the United States. The only thing is, I could be just as proud for half the money."—Arthur Godfrey

- Tax-deferred investments. These include IRAs, Keoghs, SEPs, 401(k) and 403(b) plans. Money invested in these and other qualified retirement plans grows tax-deferred until you begin tapping into the money upon retirement. At that point you pay taxes, but theoretically you'll then be in a lower tax bracket.
- Tax-deductible interest. The interest on mortgages and on most home equity loans is deductible, although interest on consumer loans and credit card debt is not.
- Charitable contributions. You can also reduce taxes by making a contribution of stocks, bonds, or other securities that have appreciated in value—you avoid the capital gains tax this way if the contribution is to an IRS-approved charity.
- Shifting income. If you have children, you can shift income to them to reduce taxes. You will want to discuss this with an accountant, for the tax benefits vary depending upon whether the child is under or over age 14 and whether the income is earned or unearned.

Tax Breaks for Adult Students
- Taking courses. If you take a course that is required either by your employer or by law, or if the course helps you maintain or improve skills that

are needed in your present job, the cost of tuition, fees, books, and necessary travel is deductible IF you file an itemized tax return.

You cannot deduct these educational expenses if you are not working or if the courses only help you qualify for a new job or new line of work, or if your employer pays the full cost.

• Child care tax credit. Another break you should know about: If you are a full-time student and your spouse is working, you may claim a tax credit for a portion of child care expenses if your child is under age 13. (A full-time student is one who attends school at least five calendar months in a year. The months do not have to run consecutively. You can attend a college, university, vocational, trade, or technical school. Correspondence schools and on-the-job training do not count.) The size of the credit depends upon the amount of care expenses involved and your income, but it ranges from 20 to 30% of up to $2,400 of care expenses for one dependent and up to $4,800 of expenses for two or more dependents. Among the expenses you can include is the amount you pay to a day care center or nursery school, but not tuition for a child in first grade or above. This credit also applies to the care of an aged or disabled dependent.

$ HINT: You do not have to itemize deductions to claim this credit, but you must file Form 2441.

• Scholarships. Scholarships and fellowships given after 1986 are tax-free only for degree candidates, and then only to the extent they pay for tuition, course-related fees, books, supplies, and equipment. Any money received for room, board, and expenses is taxable. If you are a graduate student and receive a stipend for teaching, that money is taxable and is reported by the school on Form W-2.

The Highest Tax Levy
The highest recorded personal tax levy was for $336 million on 70% of Howard Hughes' estate.

---

2 *Company Benefits*

Once you've taken care of your health and disability insurance, you can focus on other important financial benefits and company perks: retirement and savings plans, stock purchase plans, child care, and even life insurance. If you are not receiving these benefits from a company, we'll show you how to get them on your own in the next section. Let's begin with company-sponsored retirement plans.

> "I've got all the money I'll ever need—if I die by 4 o'clock."
>
> *Henny Youngman*

Company Retirement Plans

You won't die by 4 o'clock. In fact, you'll live many years. An American born in 1991 has a life expectancy of 75.5 years, with women outliving men by an average of 6.9 years.

Granted, retirement is not the first thing on your mind. It's something your grandparents may have done and your parents may be talking about. Yet that day eventually comes to all of us, and it pays to consider the future now so it will be a financially comfortable one. The rule of thumb is you'll need 70 to 80% of your salary, adjusted for inflation, to live without money worries once you stop working. Inflation is a sustained rise in the prices of most goods and services. It's now around 3%. Don't count on Social Security even though you'll be contributing for years—there's no way it can possibly meet your needs. You must have a retirement plan.

> **W.C. Fields' Definition of Inflation**
> "The cost of living has gone up another dollar a quart." (Fields, known for enjoying a drink or two, wasn't referring to milk.)

If you can't quite wrap your mind around the importance of saving now for something that will happen 35 to 40 years from now, take time to talk to your grandparents or with other retired people. Ask them to share with you what it's like living on a set income. You'll learn first hand that most older people, even those financially well off, worry about having enough money, not only for the fun things—traveling, visiting grandchildren, playing golf, spending the winter in a warmer climate—but also for making necessary home repairs, paying rent increases, or meeting escalating property taxes. And, of course, they worry both about affordable long-term care should they become seriously ill and about being a financial burden on their families.

> **Retirement Age**
> When asked why he didn't retire at the usual age of 65, comedian/movie actor George Burns said, "Retirement at 65 is ridiculous. When I was 65, I still had pimples." (Burns was in his 90s when he made this statement.)

All of these legitimate concerns should convince you to participate, to the hilt, in your company's pension plan AND to fund your IRA, every single year. The table below adds statistical fuel to the argument that, IF YOU'RE SMART, YOU'LL BEGIN BUILDING YOUR RETIREMENT NEST EGG TODAY.

> **IRA**
> Individual Retirement Account. A personal retirement account. Anyone who has earned income may contribute up to $2,000 a year to an IRA. Your contribution may or may not be tax deductible, depending upon your income and participation in other retirement plans. However, all money in your account grows on a tax-deferred basis—taxed only when you begin withdrawing funds.

Why Start Saving Now

This table shows how much you need to save each month to accumulate $500,000, assuming your money earns 10% a year.

NOTE: The required dollar amount actually triples for every decade you put off savings.

Years to Retirement	Monthly Investment Required
40	$ 79
30	219
20	653
10	2,421

(Source: American Society of Chartered Life Underwriters)

Pension Plans

Many companies have some sort of pension plan in which the employer, the employee, or both contribute money to a fund that pays out when the employee retires. However, more and more companies are shifting the burden of retirement funding from themselves to you, especially by sponsoring 401(k) plans in which the employee foots most of the cost.

If you are fortunate enough to be working for a company that has its own pension plan included in your package of fringe benefits, you should participate. Although each plan is different, they share some features in common, primarily because ERISA (see box) requires companies to conform to certain regulations in order for the employer's contributions to the plan to be tax-deductible.

 Your employer is required by law to provide you with a written description of the company's pension plan. ASK FOR IT and READ IT.

> **ERISA**
> Employee Retirement Income Security Act. A 1974 law governing the operation of the majority of private pension and benefit plans. It set up the Pension Benefit Guaranty Corporation that administers terminated plans and places liens on corporate assets for certain pension liabilities that were not funded. It covers most defined plans.

The two basic types of pension plans are defined benefit and defined contribution. In a *defined benefit plan*, the amount you receive when you retire is spelled out in advance, and the company contributes the amount necessary to fund your benefits. A *defined contribution plan* is just the opposite: the contributions to the plan are fixed, and retirement benefits are based on the returns earned on the invested contributions. (A profit-sharing plan is a defined contribution plan.)

Company pension plans typically have a professional manager who invests the contributions in stocks, bonds, mutual funds, Treasuries, and GICs.

BEING VESTED

One of the most important features of a pension plan is the point at which you become vested—when the transfer of your pension benefits to your own personal ownership, independent of your remaining with the company, is made. If you have a pension plan to which both you and your employer contribute and you leave, you are entitled to every dollar you contributed, but *until you are vested* you are not entitled to the money contributed on your behalf by your employer. The documents for your company's pension plan must spell out its vesting terms. Until the Tax Reform Act of 1986, most employees had to remain on the job ten years to vest. Now, the law gives employers two options: 1) employees must be 100% vested after five years of work; or, 2) they are given 20% vesting after three years on the job with full vesting, in graduated stages, after seven years. This new law is a great boon to you because as a younger worker you are more apt to change jobs than someone older and/or closer to retirement. It's also a blessing to men and women who take time off to have children.

IF YOU CHANGE JOBS

Before taking a different job, check on your current vesting position. Know what you will lose if you leave. You may discover that it's wise to wait until, say, you are at least 20% vested, if that is within a short time.

Keep in mind, too, that most large pension plans favor employees who stay with the company. If you job hop, even if you take pension benefits and reinvest them, you'll probably wind up with considerably less retirement income than those who stay a longer time with the firm.

If you do change jobs and you receive vested benefits, you must put them into a rollover IRA within 60 days; otherwise you'll have to pay income tax on this money *and* most likely an additional 10% tax penalty. If you don't make this rollover you can wave goodbye to much of your vested savings.

Some companies allow you to keep your vested benefits in the company's plan, even when you change jobs, until you retire. It's not easy to decide between the two options, leaving the money with your old company or moving it into a rollover IRA. To help you arrive at a decision, consider these questions:

- Will I really roll the money into an IRA or will I spend it?
- If I roll it over, can I manage the money effectively?
- Is the company's plan solid, well managed? (Check the annual report.)

Rollover IRA
A provision in the law that allows someone receiving a lump-sum payment from their company's pension plan or profit-sharing plan because of retirement or leaving the firm to roll over the money into an IRA within 60 days. The advantage: The money continues to accumulate tax-deferred until withdrawal.

Because your retirement is in the distant future, it may be tempting to spend your vested benefits if you elect to take them. It may amount to several thousand dollars (or more), which would buy that new

Subaru or pay for the trip to Europe. DON'T DO IT!
Not only will the money be gone forever, it will be
taxed. NOT SMART.

Be Sure To Read

"What You Should Know About the Pension Law"
50 cents from:

Consumer Information Center
P.O. Box 100
Attn: R. Woods
Pueblo, CO 81002

"A Guide to Understanding Your Pension Plan"
free from:

AARP
Fulfillment Center
703-550-9705

401(k) And 403(b) Plans

Many companies offer employees 40l(k) or 403(b)
retirement savings plans. These are also called "salary
reduction" plans because the percentage of your salary
that is placed in a special retirement plan is deducted
directly from your paycheck or salary.

What's Behind The Numbers?
401(k) and 403(b) plans derive their names from ob-
scure sections in the Internal Revenue Code.

401(k) plans are for the private sector.

403(b) plans are for educational institutions, hospitals, and other nonprofit organizations.

The Tax Advantages

There are some very compelling reasons to sign up for a 401(k). At the top of the list, because the amount deducted from your paycheck never appears on your W-2 form, this money escapes income taxes. Second, direct withdrawal from your paycheck means you can't get your hands on the money and fritter it away. Third, the invested money grows tax-deferred—you don't pay income tax on it until you withdraw money from the plan. Fourth, you're painlessly socking away money for retirement.

If your company has such a plan, take full advantage of it. It's one of the best tax-deferred savings plans around. Many companies sweeten the situation by matching part or all of your savings dollars, up to a certain percentage. For example, if your company contributes 50 cents for every dollar you invest, and you make $25,000 a year, here's how you come out the winner: Let's say you put 4% ($1,000) into your 401(k). Then you have to claim only $24,000 of income on your tax return. In addition, you have $1,500 (your $1,000 plus the $500 your employer contributed) in your 401(k) savings plan, rapidly growing on a tax-deferred basis—in other words, any dividends, interest, and capital gains earned are not taxed until the money is withdrawn. (Some companies even match dollar for dollar.)

How Much Can You Invest?

The annual limit on salary reduction is 15% of compensation in most plans, and there is a cap on the annual dollar amount, determined by the federal government and indexed each year to inflation.

TAPPING YOUR MONEY

Taking money out before age 59 ½ incurs a 10% tax penalty, but most plans allow employees penalty-free access to their funds through loans. You can borrow up to one-half the account balance, up to $50,000; if your loan is less than $10,000, then it may exceed half the balance. Loans must be repaid within five years, unless the money is to buy a home. The interest rate is usually just one or two percentage points above prime, but it's not tax deductible. If you fail to repay the loan within the specified time, the outstanding balance is taxable and, if you're under age 59 ½, subject to the 10% penalty.

Nearly all plans also grant "hardship" withdrawal if you absolutely have no other way to pay medical bills, meet educational expenses, or avoid eviction or mortgage foreclosure. Unless the money is used for major medical expenses, hardship withdrawals are subject to a 10% early withdrawal penalty.

The Oldest Authentic Centenarian
Shigechiyo Izumi, who lived on an island 820 miles southwest of Tokyo, lived 120 years and 237 days. He died on February 21, 1987 from pneumonia. Izumi drank Sho-chu (fire water distilled from sugar) and took up smoking at age 70. He did not have an IRA or a 40l(k) plan, but then he worked until the age of 105 and had saved his money.

WHAT TO INVEST IN

You'll have to make a decision as to where to invest your 401(k) money. Most plans offer several investment options with varying risk levels. The typical menu consists of a money market fund, several bond and stock mutual funds, GICs, and often shares in the company's stock.

> **GICs: Guaranteed Income Contract**
> A contract between an insurance company and a corporate profit-sharing or pension plan that guarantees a fixed rate of return on the invested money over the length of the contract, usually one to five years. During that time the value of your investment does not change. GICs are not insured by the government, and they are only as safe as the insurance companies that issue them. The insurance company invests GIC money in government and corporate bonds, high-yield junk bonds, mortgages, etc.

Although stocks consistently outperform bonds, GICs, and other fixed-income investments over long periods of time, most people invest their 401(k) money in GICs. They do have higher yields than money market funds and Treasury securities, but only about 0.5 to 1.5% higher, which is not much above the rate of inflation. Because you are young, you can and should take more risk than this and invest a portion of your money in a long-term stock growth fund.

 Do not overinvest your 40l(k) money in stock of the company for which you are working. Diversification is essential to sound investing, and you must never have too many eggs in one basket. Your company may be on a high roll at the moment, but what goes up often comes down, even with the bluest of the blue chip stocks. If the bottom falls out of your company, you may be out of a job; you don't want to also be out of a 401(k).

Annual Savings
Until you are 30 or 35 years old, use these guidelines for investing your 401(k) money:

Money market fund	5% to 8%
Company's stock	5% to 10%
GICs	10% to 15%
Stock fund	55% to 60%
Bond fund	25% to 30%

Company Savings Plans and Perks

Direct Deposit Plans

Your employer may offer a payroll deduction or direct deposit plan as a way to help you save. You designate how much money you want automatically deducted from your paycheck and put in a savings account or fund. (There are no tax advantages here as in a 401(k) plan.) Most credit unions and banks accept deposits from a firm's payroll department. The transfer is made electronically, so your money begins earning interest almost at once.

Subsidized Thrift Plans

In this plan, your employer typically matches your contributions, often 50 cents to your dollar, or some other amount, up to a specified maximum. The money is invested—usually in a mutual fund or an annuity—and grows until you leave the company or retire.

Stock Purchase Plans

Some companies offer employees the opportunity to buy their stock with pretax dollars, often at a discount from the market price. It can be done through payroll withholding or some other way—for instance, the corporation may contribute shares to funds that then allocate shares to employees based on their salaries.

You do not pay taxes on the value of the stock until you leave the company. In the interim, it can appreciate tax-free. If, when you receive it, you roll it into an IRA, the tax-deferred status continues.

An ESOP (Employee Stock Ownership Plan) is a great deal *IF* the stock does well, but that's never guaranteed. In 1990, for example, Pan Am declared bankruptcy, and many employees who held stock through an ESOP lost huge amounts of money. So, remember that an ESOP's success rests solely on the fortunes of the company, and it should not be confused with a retirement plan.

Profit-Sharing Plans

Another way companies link compensation to the fortunes of the firm is through profit-sharing plans. Generally employees are given a part of the firm's profits, often as a year-end cash bonus. (Often the plan stipulates that no contributions need be made during unprofitable years.)

The funds may be held in trust by the company until you leave the firm or retire. Some companies allow employees to add voluntary contributions. Taxes are typically deferred on the contributions made by the company and all the earnings in the account until withdrawn.

Other Employee Benefits
- Child care; day care center
- Gym or fitness center
- Paid tuition for you or your children
- Education loans for you or your children
- Private club privileges
- Use of company car
- Entertainment expenses
- Travel expenses
- Cost of newspapers and magazines
- Clothing or uniform allowance/cleaning costs
- Moving expenses
- Flex time
- Paid family leave

Flexible Spending Accounts for Child Care

Your company may have a special tax-free account, referred to as an FSA, that allows you to pay for child care expenses on a tax-free basis. Under the typical plan, you agree to a certain amount which is deducted from each paycheck and deposited in a separate account. As expenses are incurred, you are reimbursed from the account. The tax advantage is that the amount taken out of your salary is not subject to income or Social Security taxes, so these child care expenses are paid with pretax, not after-tax income. Salary deferrals are also free of most state and local taxes.

The Longest Pension in History
Miss Millicent Barclay, born in 1872 just three months after the death of her father, Col. William Barclay, was eligible for his military pension. She collected every single year until she died at the age of 97 in 1969. (Had she married, the pension would have ended.)

There are some drawbacks to consider.

1) You must tell your employer before the start of the year how much you want deducted from your paycheck for the coming year.

2) Any unused funds remaining in the account at the end of the year are forfeited under what the IRS calls the "use it or lose it" rule, and cannot be carried over to the next year.

Another disadvantage: Any tax-free reimbursement from an FSA reduces the expenses eligible for the dependent care tax credit.

If you are married, both you and your spouse must work in order to participate, unless your spouse is a full-time student or disabled.

The maximum annual FSA reimbursement is $2,400 per child with a maximum of two children.

Employer-Offered Insurance

Many employers provide some type of term insurance, which pays a death benefit but does not accumulate a cash value. They often do this at no cost to you. Some also give employees the option of buying additional investment-type, cash value policy. These policies are usually available at a favorable group price and have the advantage of being screened by the employer.

The Highest Life Insurance Payout
The most ever paid to a beneficiary on one person's life was some $18 million, paid on November 14, 1970 to Linda Mullendore, widow of an Oklahoma rancher. Her husband, who had been murdered, had paid $300,000 in annual premiums the year before.

Before you put money in a cash value policy at work, find out if it is portable—can you take it with you when you leave and not lose benefits?

For Your Protection

Have any policy you are considering evaluated, for $40; $30 for any additional policy by NICO (address below).

Check the insurer's A.M. Best rating; the company should provide it for you; or, look it up in Best's Insurance Reports at your library. Stick with companies rated A or above.

Ratings are also available from Standard & Poor's Corp.; 212-208-1527.

The Rule of Three

Before buying any life insurance, read these three publications *AND* talk with at least three independent agents—they sell more than one company's policies and can provide better information than an agent who works only for one insurance company.

"A Consumer's Guide to Life Insurance"
50 cents, from:

Consumer Information Center
P.O. Box 100
Attention: R. Woods
Pueblo, CO 81002

"Taking the Bite Out of Insurance" by James Hunt, $13.95, from:

National Insurance Consumer Organization (NICO)
121 North Payne Street
Alexandria, VA 22314

National Insurance Consumer Helpline,
800-942-4242

Health and Dental Insurance

You're probably healthy, strong, have boundless energy, and, other than catching the measles and an occasional bout of flu or mono, have had little need to visit a doctor. Nevertheless, an accident or unexpected illness could wipe out your savings and those of your family if you're not insured. YOU ABSOLUTELY MUST HAVE HEALTH INSURANCE no matter how healthy you are right now and WHETHER YOU'RE WORKING FULL-TIME, PART-TIME, OR ARE JOB-FREE.

Group Insurance
Most Americans get health insurance through their jobs or are covered by a family member who has insurance at work. This is called group insurance.

Premium
The dollar amount you or your employer pays for coverage; usually deducted from each paycheck if your plan is through work; the amount deducted is given on your paycheck stub.

Covered Expenses
Most insurers do not pay for all services—perhaps not for prescription drugs or mental health care, for instance. Covered services are those the insurer agrees to pay for and are listed as such in the policy.

Fee-For-Service
The old-fashioned, traditional health plan in which you choose the doctor and/or hospital. After paying a deductible, insurance covers 70 to 80% of the approved charges and you pay the rest.

Deductible
Amount paid out of pocket each year before the insurance kicks in.

HMO
A prepaid plan that provides most health care, including checkups, at a medical center and affiliated hospital for a set premium; sometimes with an additional small per-visit fee.

Primary Care Doctor
Usually your first contact for health care who monitors your health, treats minor problems, and refers you to specialists if needed. Was once called the "family doctor."

Provider
Anyone (doctor, dentist, nurse, or institution) that provides medical care.

Life Event
Any event which significantly alters your benefit needs. May include marriage, divorce, birth of a child, adoption, death of a spouse/child, your child is no longer an eligible dependent, disability, you or your spouse begin/end employment, spouse's medical benefit changes substantially, you move from full-time to part-time employment or vice versa.

Preexisting Condition
A health problem you had before becoming insured or changing insurers. Many policies will not cover preexisting conditions; others will cover them only after a waiting period. A preexisting condition may also be an illness you had treated in the past but are not currently receiving treatment for. Policies vary as to how these are defined. Some say "within five years" for example; others state "anytime in your life."

Inside Limits
This type of policy will pay only a fixed amount for your hospital room or cover surgical expenses only to a fixed amount, no matter what the actual cost. You have to pay the difference.

> **Stop-Loss Provision**
> Some major medical policies with an 80%–20% co-insurance factor will pay 100% of the eligible expenses when your out-of-pocket expenses reach a specified amount, such as $3,000.
>
> **Exclusion**
> Specific conditions or circumstances for which the policy does not provide benefits.

If You're Working Full-Time

If the company you work for has a group health plan, grab it. This is the most comprehensive and least expensive medical insurance most of us can get. As a full-time employee you are automatically eligible for company benefits. Companies with 25 or more workers are required by federal law to offer employees the chance to enroll in an HMO. In most large firms, you do not have to pass a special physical or disclose chronic illnesses to get coverage. And, your employer will pay probably 25%, 50%, or all of the annual premiums.

Some pick up a portion of the cost to insure your spouse and kids. And, a growing number include dental care as well as medical coverage. The bigger the group covered, the lower the cost of insurance to each group member. Insurance rates for group policies are set by how the group has used benefits in the past, known as an "experience rating." (Rates for individual policies are based on actuarial tables that estimate how much of the benefits individuals will use.)

Hopefully no one in your group plan suffers from Munchausen's syndrome, a continual desire to have medical treatment. One such person, William McIlloy, born in 1906, cost Britain's National Health System an estimated $4 million during his 50-year career as a patient. He tallied up 400 operations (albeit some minor ones) and stayed at 100 hospitals under 22 aliases. In 1969 he gave up this career and moved to a retirement home in Birmingham where he died in 1983.

 If your group coverage fails to provide benefits for the major portion of hospital, doctor, and surgical charges, supplement the plan on your own. For example, if your group policy pays only $200/day toward a hospital room when the cost in your area is $400/day, you need an individual policy covering most of the uncovered amount. If your group plan pays only about half the going rate for surgical procedures where you live, you'll need more coverage.

The Three Types of Health Care

There are three major health care options: conventional fee-for-service, health maintenance organizations (HMOs), and preferred provider organizations (PPOs). Your employer may offer one or a combination of these. Or, if you're purchasing your own, you have the same choices.

CONVENTIONAL PLAN

The conventional plan, also known as fee-for-service coverage, is the most expensive of the three. Here the choice of doctors and hospitals is entirely yours. The insurer only pays for part of your bills. You pay:

1. A monthly fee called a premium, often deducted from your paycheck before you see it.
2. A deductible—the amount of money you pay before the insurance payments begin.
3. Co-insurance—after paying the deductible amount for the year, you share the bill with the

insurance company. For example, you might pay 20% while the insurer pays 80%. Your portion is called co-insurance. Some plans offer a choice as to percentage of co-insurance; e.g., 50/50 or 80/20.

HMOs

An HMO is essentially a prepaid group medical service in which you are taken care of by an affiliated group of doctors who practice together and are paid a salary, not a fee for each service they perform. In exchange for a monthly premium, paid either by your employer or by you, you can use the services of these doctors, including visits, hospital stays, emergency care, surgery, lab tests, X-rays, and therapy. In some HMOs you visit a clinic where the doctors all have offices; in others, there is a loose grouping of doctors who operate out of their own individual offices. If it is a small HMO, patients are sent to specialists when necessary. There may be a small co-payment for each office visit or hospital emergency room treatment. Your medical costs are generally lower in an HMO than with fee-for-service insurance.

In almost all HMOs, you are assigned or choose one doctor to serve as your primary care doctor. He or she monitors your health and refers you to specialists. In fact, you usually cannot see a specialist without such a referral, unless you're willing to pay for it.

Preferred Provider Organizations

A preferred provider organization is a hybrid HMO and fee-for-service. An insurer or business negotiates with a limited number of doctors and hospitals to provide health care at a certain price per service. Employees are offered financial incentive to use these doctors and hospitals.

 Call your state insurance department to find out about the financial soundness and reputation of the HMO.

Comparing Health Care Options

CONVENTIONAL FEE-FOR-SERVICE

PRO:	CON:
Comprehensive	Expensive
Can choose your own doctor	Must satisfy an annual deductible
Can choose your own hospital	May need to make copayments

HEALTH MAINTENANCE ORGANIZATION

PRO:	CON:
No deductibles	Must use the HMO's doctors
Usually little or no copayment	Must use the HMO's hospitals
Premiums don't rise because you get sick	May be long waits
Premiums don't rise because use the HMO's services more	Doctors may be pressured to keep costs down and not do certain tests or send you to specialists
Few or no insurance forms to fill out	

PREFERRED PROVIDER ORGANIZATION

PRO:	CON:
Fairly comprehensive	Get reimbursed less if you go outside the network
Can go to doctors outside the network but you must pick up some of the cost	May be a deductible
	May be some copayments

Helpful hints:

1. *Avoid switching* health insurance plans if you have good coverage, if you have a chronic medical

condition, or if you have had a recent health problem. WHY? Because a new insurer may exclude coverage for any "preexisting" condition permanently if your medical problem has been serious; or for a certain time period. Even if you're in good health, many insurers now impose waiting periods or evidence of insurability on new policyholders for certain procedures.

Preexisting Conditions
Pregnancy
Alcoholism
Substance abuse
Chemical dependency
Mental or emotional disorder
Heart or circulatory problem
Cancer
Diabetes
AIDS

2. *Don't temporarily drop out* of a health plan. In fact it's always a gamble to drop coverage, even when both you and your spouse have policies. Think about it: what if only one of you is insured and the other stops work to have a baby, loses his/her job, is injured, dies, or you get a divorce. In all these cases, you'll be glad to have the double coverage.

3. *If you and your spouse* are both covered by company-sponsored insurance plans, find out which one is more generous in given areas and use it for those needs. Don't abuse the situation and make claims for the same expense under

both policies—computerized systems detect this practice and your coverage will be jeopardized.

If You Are Not Covered At Work

Not all companies offer health insurance, especially small firms; and, part-time workers are seldom covered, regardless of the size of the company.

If you're not covered at work and you cannot be added to your spouse's plan, you will need to buy your own insurance. You can get a fee-for-service, HMO, or PPO policy. Insure yourself against events that could really wreak havoc and not for every little thing that could go wrong. In other words, pay for the sore throat and runny noses out of pocket and insure against major things, such as surgery and disability.

YOUR PARENTS' PLAN

Your best bet until you are working full time is to continue coverage under your parents' health plan. Most policies cover full-time students and non-working children, although the cut-off age is anywhere from 19 to 23.

 If you are covered under your parents' group plan, COBRA regulations allow you to continue in the plan for up to 18 months until you find a job that offers you your own insurance. If you have a preexisting condition, it will be covered.

In some states you can convert coverage under a family policy to an individual policy, although the new policy will be costly and you may not get the same range of benefits.

STUDENT HEALTH PLANS

Often graduate and undergraduate students can get basic coverage through a school-sponsored plan.

However, you can also use the school's clinic for simple basic needs, such as shots, birth control, and counseling. Fees are usually modest.

GAP POLICIES

If you are not covered either by your parents' plan or by a student health plan, you can buy a short-term policy to take care of the gap between jobs, or between graduation and your first position. If you decide to travel prior to taking a job, make certain coverage applies outside the country; many short-term policies apply only to U.S. doctors, clinics, and hospitals.

Some Financially-Solvent Health Insurers	Company Rating
State Farm Life	A+
Jefferson-Pilot Life	A+
Northwestern Mutual Life	A+
Country Life	A+
United Ins. Co. of America	A+
Guardian Life	A+
Continental Asr.	A+
New York Life	A+
Hartford Life	A+
Franklin Life	A-

(Companies with more than $2 billion in total assets)
Source: Weiss Research Inc., 2200 N. Florida Mango Road, West Palm Beach, FL 33409.

Short-term policies are available in every state and typically run 60 to 180 days and can be renewed, but only once. They do not cover preexisting conditions, pregnancy, or outpatient therapy, but are easy to get:

With most you simply fill out a form and send in a check. Although premiums are fairly low, companies often require that they be paid in one lump sum, rather than monthly. Deductibles range from $250 to $2,500, occasionally to $5,000.

 Pick a policy with a pro-rated refund for the unused portion that kicks in if you find work before coverage ends.

Three companies currently selling gap polices:

Golden Rule, 317-297-4123
Time Insurance, 414-271-3011
Bankers Life & Casualty, 203-683-0709

ASSOCIATION AND GROUP INSURANCE

If you cannot get health insurance benefits through regular employment, if you are unable to convert a group policy to an individual one when you leave a job, or you are not covered by a student plan, you may be able to purchase group insurance through an association. The most common groups offering insurance to their members are college alumni associations, trade and professional associations (such as a local bar association, journalists/writers groups, or an engineer's society), business groups, labor unions, and civic organizations. This type of insurance is usually cheaper than buying coverage on your own because the group can negotiate a better discount from an insurer than an individual.

BLUE CROSS/BLUE SHIELD

If you cannot find a group to join, or you want to supplement the coverage you're receiving through your
company, you'll have to bite the bullet and buy insurance—either from a commercial insurer or from your
local Blue Cross/Blue Shield. Be prepared for monthly
premiums between $100 and $200. (Blue Cross covers
hospital costs, while bills for medical and surgical needs
are taken care of by Blue Shield.) Although the "Blues"
exist throughout the entire country, local plans are au-
tonomous and offer different coverage.

The Blues
The first Blue Cross program was established at Baylor
University Hospital in Dallas in 1929. It covered a small
group of teachers for 21 days of hospital care. The
monthly premium was 50 cents per teacher.

The "Blues" usually provide coverage at cheaper rates than the Aetnas and John Hancocks, because as nonprofit organizations they are exempt from certain taxes and can negotiate lower fees with doctors and hospitals. They charge premiums as do other insurance companies, but they pay bills directly to the hospital. (With commercial insurance you often have to pay the bill and wait to be reimbursed, and your reimbursement may or may not cover the full bill.) Most pay 100% of each bill, not just 80 or 85% as is common with the for-profit insurers. Blue Cross/Blue Shield policies are guaranteed to be renewable, which is not always the case with commercial insurance.

A number of the Blues, including New York State's, let you sign up for coverage regardless of your health, during a period called open enrollment. So, if you have a chronic medical condition, the Blues may be your only choice.

Types of Coverage

When looking at fee-for-service policies there are three types of coverage to consider: basic protection, major medical, and disability.

BASIC PROTECTION

Basic protection includes benefits while in the hospital, including pay toward daily room and board, regular nursing services while in the hospital, and certain services and supplies, such as X-rays, lab tests, drugs, and medication. It also pays toward the costs of surgical procedures, related doctor visits, doctor's fees during hospitalization, and some diagnostic and lab tests.

Major Medical

Major medical covers long-term illness or injury by helping to pay for just about everything prescribed by your doctor. It takes over, in a way, where your basic coverage cuts off, continuing treatment inside and outside a hospital. It is usually coordinated with a basic policy so that there's no duplication. Most major medical policies pay for doctors including specialists, osteopathy, and chiropractors as well as drugs when prescribed. Major medical policies can be purchased alone or in conjunction with basic protection. The deductible may run anywhere from $250 to $1,000 to $5,000 or more, and the higher the deductible you are willing to accept, the lower the cost of your insurance. Of course, if your major medical is provided by your employer, the deductible is what he determines. In addition to a deductible, these policies all have something called "coinsurance"—that part of the medical costs you are obligated to pay with your insurer—most major medical plans pay 75 to 85% of all eligible medical costs above the deductible, and you pay the remainder. Many policies where you pay a share of the costs have a "stop-loss" provision, so you only have to pay up to a certain amount and no more.

Disability Income

Disability income insurance assures a regular cash income in case of disability through illness or injury. You collect a percentage of your former earnings until you can return to work. Most require that you be totally disabled before benefits begin—some policies define disability merely as being unable to do your regular work; others are tougher. Policies pay benefits starting anywhere from a week to six months after the onset of disability. The longer you wait, the lower your premium. Benefits extend from as few as 13 weeks to as long as a lifetime. The shorter the benefit period, the lower the premium. The maximum most insurers will pay is two-thirds of your annual gross salary.

"The Consumer's Guide to Disability Insurance"
Helps you decide if you need coverage and how to compare policies. Free from:

Health Insurance Association of America
    Box 41455
    Washington, DC 20018

If you become disabled, you also become eligible for Medicare. That means you want a policy that will pay costs "over and above" what Medicare will pay.

When You Change Jobs

If you leave your job, are fired, or laid off and the company has more than twenty workers, your employer must let you continue your health coverage under the company's plan for up to 18 months after you leave under COBRA. This also applies if you divorce and are covered under your spouse's plan. You will have to pay the premiums, but your old employer must offer you the continuation coverage at his cost. That cost is always cheaper than taking out an individual policy. This ruling also applies if you are cut back to part-time status.

If at the end of 18 months, when the group extension expires, you don't have a job with health benefits, your old employer must offer you continued coverage but at the far pricier individual rates. Still, TAKE IT. On the other hand, if you have arranged for new

> **COBRA Exceptions**
> Not everyone is protected by this rule: The federal gov-
> ernment, firms with fewer than 20 employees, and
> church groups are exempt.

coverage, don't leave your current coverage until the
new policy kicks in—and that date may not be the
same as when you sign up or pay your first premium.

> **To Learn More**
>
> "A Consumer's Guide to Health Maintenance Orga-
> nizations" ($4)
>
> *National Consumer's League (202-639-8140)*
> 815 15th Street N.W.
> Suite 928
> Washington, DC 20005
>
> "Buyer's Guide to Insurance" ($3)
>
> *National Consumer Insurance Organization
> (703-549-8050)*
> 121 North Payne Street
> Alexandria, VA 22314
>
> National Insurance Consumer Helpline
> (800-942-4242)
>
> Help and info on choosing an agent, insurer, CO-
> BRA, disability, managed care plans, etc.

3 *Your Second Job*

This may be a slight exaggeration on Confucius' part, but it is true that if you like what you're doing, doing it won't be a burden. If you don't like what you're doing, or the amount you're being paid, then it's up to you to change it. And change is what this chapter is all about—and the fact that you don't have to stay in a job or career until you're old and gray. Plenty of successful people, like Wally Amos, began in one field only to wind up in another. Wally, a successful Los Angeles talent scout, left show biz to open a chocolate chip cookie store in the late 1970s. He had always loved his Aunt Della's cookies and instinctively thought others would, too. Within five years his Famous Amos cookies had become a household name, bringing in revenues of more than $5 million a year.

This chapter is also about your decision to take on new challenges, assume more responsibility, to accept that offer of a transfer from your current employer or to take a new job. You'll also learn exactly how to get more money in the process and take tax deductions for some of your career-shifting expenses.

> "Choose a job you love, and you will never have to work a day in your life."
>
> *Confucius*

How to Move Up Within the Company

There are certain advantages to staying with a job for several years, even while you're in your 20s or early 30s. It pays to hang in there long enough to be vested and to take advantage of employee-paid education or other benefits. It is also seen as a mark of stability and commitment if you don't job jump every year or two. However, it's not to your advantage to remain in a job where you are unhappy, where advancement is not possible, where it's likely you'll be fired or laid off.

True Job Stability
The record for the longest working career, which lasted 98 years, is held by Mr. S. Izumi, who began as an employee in a Japanese sugar mill in 1872 and retired as a sugar cane farmer in 1970 at the age of 105.

But first, let's address moving up to a better position within the firm and, in the process, getting a raise.

If your company has reorganized or had a series of layoffs, and you're still on board, this is a good time to go for an in-house promotion. The so-called dead wood—those that didn't enhance the company, have been cut. Look for those areas where additional help and ideas are needed—perhaps because work has backed up, there's no one to head a particular project, or a department is simply overwhelmed with work. Once you identify these specific needs, suggest to management what you can do to fill in, to make things better for the firm.

If someone has been reassigned, don't wait for the position to be advertised—if you think you're right for the vacancy, speak to the person in charge, express your interest, and be specific about why you are qualified for the job.

You may not get the first in-house promotion you go after, but never mind. Your action will capture management's attention and clearly demonstrate that you're thinking, on the ball, ambitious, and flexible—all of which eventually may be reflected in a better position and more pay.

Getting a Raise or Promotion

Here are six strategies for getting a raise and/or promotion:

1. *Get* the facts. When you ask for a raise, don't simply pick a number or percentage out of the air. Find out what other companies are paying for similar work. Make a written list of three to five.

2. *Schedule* a meeting with your boss. But don't just pick any old date. Time the meeting to follow some task you performed well, something for which you received praise, or after volunteering to take on an extra assignment.

3. *List* your accomplishments on paper. These could include: how much money you've *saved* the company or your department; how you've *increased* productivity; how you *brought* favorable publicity to the firm; how you *rescued* a poor situation; how you've *improved* customer or client relations.

4. *Add* supporting documentation, such as sales records, reports, letters of congratulations, etc.

5. *Showcase* your ideas in the meeting. Tell what you plan to do for the company over the next three, six, or twelve months. List your ideas on paper and have extra copies to distribute.

6. *Wind up* your presentation fairly quickly. Don't rattle on. If you're told that a raise is not possible right now, ask when it might be possible.

In Lieu of a Raise

If your employer hands out a litany of reasons why a raise isn't possible, such as the company is going through belt-tightening or all raises have been frozen, bargain for something other than money. Using your own good judgment, ask for:

- an extra week's vacation
- a Friday or a Monday off every month
- tuition for a degree or certificate program
- expenses to attend professional meetings and seminars
- expenses to attend an out-of-town convention
- child care or some other benefit
- time to work at home one or two days a week and the equipment necessary (computer, fax, etc.)

 Make certain you bargain only for benefits or extras that are really meaningful to you; spell out why they are.

Taking Financial Advantage of Your Age

In today's world of mergers, acquisitions, takeovers, sell-offs, and downsizing, nothing is a sure thing. An office shake-up is inevitable for most of us sooner or later. Yet, you can come out ahead rather than behind—because you are young compared with others in your office, you are also probably paid less than senior employees and executives. That makes you attractive to the new management.

> **Young Workers Who Were Well Paid**
>
> - The youngest person to accumulate a million dollars was the child actor Jackie Coogan. He co-starred with Charlie Chaplin in *The Kid* in 1920.
> - The youngest billionaire in the United States was William Gates, cofounder of Microsoft. He was 20 when he set up his company and was a billionaire by 31.
> - The youngest living millionairess is Shirley Temple, now Mrs. Charles Black. She earned over $1 million before she was 10.

Younger workers are also viewed as being more flexible, willing to accept different assignments, and even move to new locations if need be. They also tend to be less rigid than older employees when it comes to learning new skills. Let the new boss know that you're willing to not only go with the flow, but make changes as required.

An office shakeup also creates vacancies, one of which you may be able to fill. In this way you may actually land your first managerial position, be asked to work on a team project, or take over an empty position.

Lateral Moves

Although lateral moves are not promotions, they can be financially and professionally to your advantage—*IF* they help you gain valuable experience, more comprehensive knowledge of your company and your industry. They are often an excellent solution if you're boxed in, if your job is at a dead end, or if you want to learn all there is about a field. Yet not all lateral moves are positive. The greatest pitfall is that you will wind up simply repeating your skills and experience while sitting at a new desk. Just say "no" to such an offer.

When To Move On

Before making any job move, up, down, or sideways, ask yourself: Where do I want to be 5, 10, even 15 years from now? You may have specific career goals in mind, or simply a vague notion of what your dreams are. If you want to run a large corporation, head a research team, be a political leader, or work part time while writing The Great American Novel, you need to factor into work-related decisions these hopes and aspirations.

You also need to consider your plans for parenthood, if any—when (and if) you want to have children. What type of job complements being a parent? How will children affect your career development? Will you want to take time out, and if so, for how long, when you have children? Are you in a field in which you can do that? If you're a hot shot, a hard worker, a successful networker, in the right place at the right time, you may be offered a job with another company even if you don't go after it. Should you accept? Yes, if it's one you would have sought on your own. Yes, if it's a clear promotion and/or you're getting at least a 20% pay increase. If it's simply a lateral move and you'll be vested within a year or year and a half, you should wait for a vertical move.

Three other considerations: Is the salary at market-level? What will you learn in the new position that will help you get the next job or promotion? Is it a good company—better than the one for which you're working?

Looking for a New Job
There are plenty of good books on job hunting, resume writing, and interviewing techniques (see sidebar) so we'll highlight only the key points you may
have overlooked. Then, since the focus of this book is
your finances, we'll also discuss some job hunting expenses that may be tax deductible.

Where the Jobs Are
According to the Bureau of Labor Statistics, these occu-
pations are expected to gain large numbers of jobs
between now and 2005:

Systems analysts/computer scientists

Computer programmers

Child-care workers

Receptionists and information clerks

Registered nurses

Nursing aides/orderlies/attendants

Restaurant chefs/cooks

Lawyers

Accountants/auditors

Guards

Airline pilots/mechanics

Automobile mechanics

Dietitians/nutritionists

Farm managers

Veterinarians

Occupational therapists

Nurses

Optometrists/ophthalmologists

Physical therapists

More Job Info

The Occupational Outlook Handbook, published every two years by the U.S. Department of Labor's Bureau of Labor Statistics. Your library should have a copy, or order one from the Superintendent of Documents, U.S. Government Printing Office, Box 371954, Pittsburgh, PA 15250, $23. It contains enormous amounts of information on each occupation, including salaries, requirements, job outlook, and what the job is like.

The Harvard Guide to Careers, published by the Office of Career Services, Harvard University, 55 Dunster St., Cambridge, MA 02138; 1991; $10 plus $2 shipping.

Seven Job-Hunting Tips

It's a pretty tight job market, with unemployment rates high and major corporations cutting back on full-time employees. In addition to having a sharp-looking resume, going after every lead, and networking round the clock, here are seven insider tips you may have overlooked:

1. *Get in the door.* If the firm you'd like to work for doesn't have an opening or isn't offering you the position you want, consider taking a different job, even one on a lower level, to get your foot in the door. Once there, you can demonstrate your abilities and commitment.

2. *Be a volunteer or intern.* Some companies and many nonprofit organizations let people learn, as nonpaid volunteers or interns. If you're well suited to the work, you may indeed land a paying position.

3. *Be flexible.* If you can live somewhere else, work odd hours, be amenable to assignments, you open the door to many more job possibilities.

4. *Talk with parents, stepparents, and other relatives.* Sometimes excellent sources of information about job openings are right within our immediate families. Ask yours for a list of friends and business associates who could be helpful and then follow up by writing or calling them. (Don't be too proud or stubborn about "doing it on your own"; that's short-sighted.)

5. *Look to smaller companies.* They have been picking up the slack due to the huge number of large companies that have laid off employees.

6. *Think temporary.* Take short-term assignments; fill in for someone sick, on vacation or maternity leave. It may lead to a full-time job, or you may find that you like the variety. More and more companies are using professional temp agencies as a source of workers—engineers, lawyers, consultants, paralegals, paramedics, plant managers, computer and word processing experts. Temping is no longer the exclusive province of office workers.

7. *Start your own business.* Although this is very appealing and exciting to anyone with entrepreneurial instincts, look before you leap, and don't proceed without reading the rest of this chapter.

Looking for a Job by Computer
These job search programs tell the addresses of firms, how to negotiate your salary, etc.:

Individual Software's *ResumeMaker,* disk plus easy-to-follow handbook helps you compose cover letters.

Scope International's *Jobhunt* program gives names, addresses, and info on 600+ employers, arranged by job type and geographic region.

Tax Breaks for Job Hunters

If you itemize your deductions on your tax return, you may deduct some of the expenses of looking for a new job as long as it is in the *same line of work*, whether or not you actually find a new job. The deduction is subject to the 2% AGI floor.

 The expenses of looking for a job in a different line of work are not deductible, even if you land the job.

In all cases, keep careful records and all receipts and canceled checks, and put them in a separate file. These expenses are generally deductible:

- transit fares and car expenses for traveling to and from job interviews
- cost of preparing and mailing resumes, stamps, stationery, fax transmissions
- employment agency fees
- executive recruiter fees
- telephone calls regarding a job search
- employment-related education

TRAVEL EXPENSES

If you travel to find a new job in the same line of work, you may deduct travel expenses including living costs. Let's say you travel to another city for an interview and at the same time visit a friend there; you may still deduct the cost of transportation provided the trip was primarily related to your job search.

If You Move to a New Location

You may deduct expenses incurred in moving to a new job location for:

1. The cost of moving your household goods and personal possessions; and
2. Travel and lodging costs during the move.

Under the Tax Act of 1993, you can no longer deduct the cost of selling your old home or purchasing a new one, any meal expenses incurred in pre-move house-hunting trips, or the cost of temporary lodging *after* landing a job.

THE DISTANCE TEST

To deduct moving expenses, you must meet what the IRS calls a 50-mile distance test. The distance between your new job location and your old home must be at least 50 miles more than the distance between your old job location and your old home. Use this worksheet to sort it out:

Worksheet

Distance between:	Miles
Your old residence and new job location	____
Your old residence and old job location	____
The difference (must be at least 50 miles)	____

THE TIME TEST

In addition to meeting the 50-mile distance test, you must stay in the new locality and work full time for at least 39 weeks during the first 12 months after your move. However, you don't need to work 39 consecutive weeks nor stay with the same boss—you can actually change jobs provided you stay in the same area for the 39 weeks. If you lose your job, this requirement is waived—unless you were fired because of misconduct or you resign.

 Newlyweds, you may be able to claim a tax break for moving in together. . .if you lived in different cities but after getting married one of you moved to the other's city and got a job.

When You Land A New Job

If you decide to leave your current job for a new one, you want the transition to be a smooth one.

First, give at least two weeks notice, longer if possible.

Second, write a gracious letter of resignation to your boss, mentioning that you've learned a great deal from your time with the company and that you've enjoyed working with him/her and the other people in the organization. As you compose this letter of resignation, keep in mind that you want to be able to ask your ex-boss for a letter of reference and to call upon him/her or other co-workers in the future. After all, the person that sat in the office next to you may some day be head of a company you'd like to work for.

Third, check with your benefits office(r) regarding the transfer of any pension benefits.

Fourth, if you have been given a farewell party or a going away gift from a group or individuals, be certain to write to each person involved, thanking them for their thoughtfulness.

A Checklist for Moving Day

When you do move, you'll find there are a host of details to handle, especially if you're moving out of town. The actual day always arrives too soon, no matter how organized you are. This checklist will help you keep your financial life in order. Begin it one to two months before M-Day.

- *Open* a checking account in your new town—in person or by mail, about a month ahead. Once you have an address, order printed checks. You can mail a check to open the account, but first ask if it needs to be a certified or cashier's check. Then, just prior to moving, have your old bank wire the balance on hand to the new bank.

 Ask your new bank if they have a newcomer's service—brochures on the bank's services, local information, discounts, etc.

- *Close* out all old bank accounts, taking care that all checks have cleared before folding your checking account. Close money market accounts and savings accounts after your last interest has been credited. Give your old bank your new address and, of course, the name and address of your new bank.

- *Get* copies of your dental and medical records, X-rays, and test results to avoid paying for duplicates with a new doctor or HMO.

- *Inventory* your possessions before they are packed. Record serial numbers of appliances and equipment; videotape or photograph antiques, collections, jewelry, and artwork. Keep the inventory and pictures with other important papers.

- *Gather* critical papers—insurance documents, stock and bond certificates, safe deposit items, household inventory—and put them in a portable metal box that can be locked. Take it in person to your new home. Do not entrust it to the movers. Alternative: Send it by insured certified mail to your new office, or pick it up at your new post office. (The post office will hold certified mail for 15 days and insured mail for 30 days.) Make photocopies of all documents you mail; mail the copies separately or take them with you.

- *Get* your professional license. If you need to take a licensing test, bar exam, or register a new business, check with state and local officials well in advance of your move. Find out about special laws affecting running a business from your home. This type of red tape is time consuming and can delay collecting income.

- *Get* a driver's license application and car registration form, if you move to a new state.

- *Notify* the post office, phone company, and utilities of your change of address.

- *Take* enough travelers' checks to cover your expenses for the first week or two in case your new checks are not printed in time.

- *Switch* any automatic investment and savings programs to your new bank.

- *Give* your new address to your stockbroker, lawyer, accountant, financial planner, insurance agent, mutual fund companies, credit card companies, and any lenders.

- *Check* with your insurance agent about coverage while moving, including items you carry in your car or by plane or train.

- *Tell* the IRS where you will be living. Call 800-829-3676.
- *Call* your old state's tax division and get directions for filing any forms once you've moved.
- *Revise* your will and other legal documents if your move is out of state.
- *Get* several quotes on your auto insurance; a move from a small town to a city or to a rural area or vice versa necessitates differing types of coverage.

PART TWO

Your Salary

Now that you're earning money, getting a paycheck, it's important not to spend every penny of it—something that's amazingly easy to do. In Part II you'll find out how to keep your spending within reason and not pile up huge credit card charges. We'll also look at when, where and how to borrow money, handle old college loans and launch a simple stress-free savings plan.

"I've been rich and I've been poor; rich is better."

Sophie Tucker

4 *Using a Bank or Credit Union*

Although bank interest rates have been notoriously low the last few years, with savings accounts and CDs yields hovering between 2 and 5.5%, you may well wonder if you need a bank. Yet, as Willie Sutton said when asked by a reporter why he robbed banks, "that's where the money is." Where else can you get a safe deposit box, a mortgage, a checking account, a savings account, a personal loan, travelers' checks, and access to a cash machine under one roof? Many banks also sell shares of stocks and mutual funds. If you have enough money, you can get a "bundled account" that links checking, savings, CDs, IRAs, and your brokerage account onto one monthly statement. And if you have even more money, you may qualify for private banking and be assigned a personal banker. Nevertheless, as Willie knew full well, there are lots of differences between banks, and it pays to pick the right one.

"A bank is a place that will lend you money if you can prove you don't need it."

Bob Hope

Picking the Right Bank

You're just out of school. You've started a new job, and you need to begin paying some bills. The big question is, where should you open your checking account?

The first thing to realize about a bank is that it's in business to make money. It sells a number of services for which you pay. How much you pay depends upon the amount of time you're willing to spend investigating different institutions and their fees. The seductive convenience of using the bank on the nearest corner is no longer the only criterion for picking a bank. You also need to consider services (which have proliferated), costs (which have steadily been rising), financial stability (you know many banks have failed recently), and, of course, whether there are incredibly long lines at lunch time. At the end of this section you'll find a list of questions to ask potential bankers; visit or call several, compare their answers, and then make your final decision.

The Advantages of Consolidation

You may be thinking about opening accounts at several banks—perhaps because one is nearby, another has higher rates, and a third, longer hours. That's the approach taken by the comic W.C. Fields. He had 700 accounts in banks all over the world, so that if he was ever stranded somewhere, he'd have cash. Fields also worried constantly about being penniless and starving to death. The 700 bank accounts helped dilute his fear. When he died on Christmas Day, 1946, his executors found only 30 of the 700 accounts. Although many were in his own name, he also used fictitious ones, such as Figley E. Whitesides, Sneed Hearn, Dr. Otis Guelpe, and Professor Curtis T. Bascom. Fields left his money to establish an orphanage "Where no religion of any sort is to be preached." I don't recommend that you follow his example, amusing as it may be. Open no more than one or two accounts, and have them in your legal name. With the proliferation of ATMs (described below), you'll be able to get cash almost anywhere in the world.

There are in fact real pluses to doing all your banking at one institution (this is called "relationship banking"). Banks impose stiff fees on most types of accounts, and about the only way to avoid or reduce them is to keep a certain amount of money in the bank. It pays, not only to shop around but to consolidate—you may find a bank that waives fees for customers who keep more than one account at the bank and whose combined balances exceed the minimums.

 One of the first banks to investigate is the one your employer uses—you may find it easier (or at least faster) to open an account there, and most likely you'll be given special consideration.

Other reasons for consolidation: It makes you more important to the bank, so you are likely to get preferential treatment such as immediate crediting of your deposits and overdraft privileges. If you gain a reputation as a good customer, it will ease the way to getting a loan. Larger account balances also often earn higher yields. And if you are establishing credit for the first time, it may help you get a bank credit card if you have an account (or several) at that institution.

> "If you would like to know the value of money, go and try to borrow some."—Benjamin Franklin

Savings Accounts

Banks offer three basic types of savings accounts: the old-fashioned passbook account, the newer statement account, and a money market deposit account. Rates on all three are low, but offsetting that disadvantage—your accounts have liquidity and your money is safe, provided your account is fully federally insured.

Liquidity
Refers to assets that easily and quickly can be converted into cash without substantial loss, such as savings and checking accounts.

In a *passbook account* all deposits, withdrawals, and interest paid are recorded in a little book, which you bring with you to the bank when conducting a transaction. In a *statement account* these same transactions are recorded electronically and sent to you in a monthly or quarterly printout. *Money market deposit accounts* have slightly higher yields, higher minimum deposit requirements, and offer limited check-writing privileges. (Do not confuse these with money market mutual funds, which have higher yields and are described in Chapter 7.) Typically, you can write up to three checks per month for free. MMDAs are a good place to park money because they earn interest but then move it on to a higher yielding investment.

Why bother with a savings account if rates are so low and higher ones are available with a money market mutual fund? For one reason, the minimum opening requirements are lower than for money market mutual funds. If you have less than $250 with which to start your savings account, a bank is just about your only choice. Three additional advantages: your money has liquidity, is even available 24 hours a day if you have an ATM card, and it's safe if fully federally insured.

Federal Reserve

Our central banking system consisting of 12 regional Reserve banks throughout the country. Each acts as a central banker for the private banks in its area, holding money reserves, providing cash, granting loans to member banks, and other services. There are also a number of branches. Call the one nearest you to find out about a tour.

The Big Twelve

Boston	Chicago
New York	St. Louis
Philadelphia	Minneapolis
Cleveland	Kansas City
Richmond	Dallas
Atlanta	San Francisco

Don't lose your savings account. To avoid becoming a lost depositor, every year make a deposit or withdrawal or take in your passbook and get interest credited. If you become an inactive account (the time length varies from state to state), your money will be turned over to the state.

Checking Accounts

The other primary reason most of us use banks is to write checks to pay bills. Most banks charge for checks, although if you have a large enough balance or a certain type of checking account, you may get free checking, at least for a while.

Get Low-Cost Checks
You can order personalized checks for less than what your bank charges from:

Checks in the Mail, 800-733-4443

Custom Direct, 800-272-5432

To reduce the cost of check writing, pay large bills ($250 or $500) from a money market deposit account or mutual fund.

The three basic types of checking accounts are a regular account, a special account, and a NOW account (negotiated order of withdrawal). Individual banks may give these accounts their own names and regulations, but in general: a *regular checking account* usually does not charge for checks nor does it pay interest; with many, there's a small monthly fee. A *NOW account* pays interest and typically requires at least $500 to open; there be may service fees and a required minimum to avoid penalties. *Special accounts* typically have no minimum balance requirement but charge a per-check fee and often a monthly fee; they are intended for those who write very few checks.

Special Checks
- Travelers' checks. Issued as a convenience to customers and sold for a nominal fee. If they are lost or stolen, you get your money back.
- Certified checks. A personal check that has been stamped "certified" by the bank after the funds have been set aside from your account to cover the full amount of this check. Used when buying a house and often as rent security.
- Cashier's checks. If you don't have a checking account but need a guarantee of payment, you can give the bank money and it will make out a cashier's check to the person you designate.
- Money orders. Similar in appearance to a check, they have the name of the purchaser, the name of the person or company who is to receive the money, and the amount to be paid. To get a money order, give the bank (or post office) cash for the amount plus a small fee. It is a simple way to transfer small amounts of money without using a check or cash.

Compare Bank Fees

Study these median fees for bank checking accounts and see if you're paying too much at your bank.

- Non-Interest Bearing Checking
  Account
  Monthly fee — $4.50 to $5.50
  Minimum balance to waive fees — $500
  Average balance to waive fees — $775 to $1,000
- Interest-Bearing Checking Account
  Monthly fee — $6.25 to $8.00
  Minimum balance to waive fees — $1,000
  Average balance to waive fees — $1,500 to $2,000
  Interest rate — 2.45%
- Automated Teller Machines
  ATM fee at bank's own machine — $0.00 to $0.25
  ATM fee at another bank's machine — $0.00 to $2.00

(Source: American Bankers Association)

Questions to Ask Prospective Banks/Bankers

- How much do you charge for checks?
- Is there any way I can get free checking?
- What interest rate do you pay on checking accounts?
- How much do I need to open a checking, savings, money market deposit account? What minimum must I maintain for each of these?
- What is the penalty if I fall below the minimum?
- How is interest computed? How frequently?
- What do you charge for bounced checks?
- What is the interest rate on overdraft protection?
- What do you charge if I use my ATM card at another bank?
- How much of my money will be insured?

- How long for local checks to clear? Out of town checks?
- If I put $250 in a savings account, how much will I have in one year? In a money market deposit account?

Other Bank Goodies

OVERDRAFT PROTECTION

Though you may think you'll never bounce a check, and maybe you won't, it does happen even to the most cautious—a check may not have cleared in time, you miscalculated your account balance, you forgot to write in the amount of a check written earlier in the month.

Overdraft
A check drawn on an account that does not have enough money to cover it.

If you have overdraft protection, your account will be bounce-proof, and you'll save the service fee for checks returned because of insufficient funds, which averages about $15. This is a line of credit that you must apply for just as you would a credit card. It is an automatic loan if you overdraw your checking account. The service is free until you use it; then there are interest charges. Some banks automatically repay the loan from your next deposit; others deduct only a portion. ASK.

Take care not to abuse this coverage and write bad checks, using your overdraft protection as a credit line. You'll wind up paying the bank about 18% for the privilege.

ATM Guidelines

- Pick a PIN you can remember so you won't have to write it down. Do not carry it in your wallet, and do not share it with friends. Do not use your birthdate or address or anything a crook could figure out from the documents in your wallet.

- Enter each ATM transaction in your checkbook. Keep the machine-issued transaction slips.

- If you deposit cash, check the transaction slip at the same time. If the machine made an error in recording the amount deposited, report it as soon as possible.

- Be cautious about withdrawing cash from an ATM at night, on weekends, or when the area is deserted.

- Visa and MasterCard can be used in many ATMs for cash advances. In most cases you wind up paying interest on these advances from the minute you receive them.

- Banks set a limit on how much cash can be withdrawn in any one day. If you're getting cash for a trip, find out the daily limit well in advance.

ATM CARDS

There's absolutely no question that these plastic cards which you slide into a bank's automatic teller machine to get instant cash are handy. Not only are bank ATMs open after the bank closes, through regional and national networks you can get money when traveling, even abroad. By tapping in your PIN (personal identification number) on a key pad you can find out how much is in your account, make deposits, withdrawals, and in some cases move money from one account to another.

ATMs, however, can be a bit too handy: You may

find yourself spending more because it's so easy to run to the cash machine at lunchtime, after work, or on weekends when you're out of funds rather than sticking to your budget, and you can run up fees when using your card in certain networks.

ATM Mistakes
Write to your bank as soon as you receive your statement. By law the bank must resolve your complaint with 45 days of receiving your letter. If problem persists, contact:

Federal Reserve Board Consumer Affairs
    20th and C Street, NW
    Washington, DC 20551

 If you feel out of control, make it a habit to get the amount of cash you need just once a week and leave your ATM card at home the rest of the time.

STOPPING A CHECK

If you need to stop payment on a check, perhaps because you've signed up for a nine-year subscription to a magazine you don't really want, you've had second thoughts about a purchase, you don't have enough money in your account to cover the check, or because a check has been lost or stolen, follow these steps. First, if it's because you've changed your mind about a purchase, write to the company indicating this fact. The federal consumer protection law gives you three days, after a purchase in your home, to reverse your decision and cancel a contract. Second, in all cases, notify the bank, first by telephone and then in writing. Give the bank the date of the check, the amount, and the name of the payee. The bank will not release money if the check is presented for collection. Most charge $10 to $25 per checked stopped.

 Ask how long stop payment is in effect; you may need to extend it.

SAFE DEPOSIT BOXES

These metal boxes, located in a bank's vault, are for storing valuables. They come in several sizes and are rented for an annual fee. Only the person who has signed the signature card with the bank and has the key to open the box may open the box. It takes two keys to do so—the renter has one and the bank the other; neither key will work alone. Among the items kept in safe deposit boxes:

stock and bond certificates

deed to house

birth certificates

copies of wills

marriage/divorce certificates

jewelry

proof of valuables: such as pictures of heirlooms, antiques, and artwork

Do not keep items that might be needed should the person who rents the box die, such as his/her will, life insurance policies, cemetery deed or burial instructions. The box may be sealed shut upon the death of the owner. State rules vary, so check first before putting vital documents in a box.

Insuring Your Money

To be safe, only keep your money in a bank that insures its deposit through the Federal Deposit Insurance Corporation (FDIC), an independent government agency. (Most banks are FDIC-insured, but always check first.) Coverage is up to $100,000 per person (not per account) at any one bank. If you have several savings accounts, even at different branches, and they are all in the same name, they are lumped together for insurance coverage. In other words, if you have four $100,000 accounts in the same name in one institution, you are insured for a total of $100,000, not $400,000. The $100,000 figure applies to both principal and interest. And, bear in mind that if you have money in a checking account, a savings account, a money market deposit account, and a CD, you do not get $100,000 of insurance for each account, you get only a total coverage of $100,000. You can expand coverage through joint accounts; ask your banker for details. And, if your have an IRA at a bank, any money market deposit accounts or CDs in it are insured separately. For more information, call the FDIC consumer hot line: 800-934-3342.

What a Difference $1,000 Makes

If you save $1,000 a year (that's less than $20 a week), you can quickly build a sizable nest egg. This table assumes you invest that $1,000 at the beginning of each year. Taxes will reduce your holdings unless you save in a tax-exempt investment or through a tax-deferred plan, such as your IRA.

Annual Interest Rate	20 Yrs.	10 Yrs.	5 Yrs.
5%	$33,775	$13,134	$5,794
6%	38,993	13,972	5,975
7%	44,211	14,810	6,156
8%	49,423	15,645	6,335

(Source: Case Western Reserve Univ.)

Advantages of Credit Unions

Contrary to popular opinion, a credit union is not a labor union. It is a consumer-owned, not-for-profit cooperative. Many are founded by labor unions but others by corporations, colleges, universities, and other groups. They are open only to members and employees and their families. Credit unions provide checking and savings accounts, loans, and other financial services for members. Because they are not-for-profit and run by members, their overhead is low and they almost always pay higher interest rates on accounts and charge lower rates on loans. Service fees also tend to be below those of banks. Most are federally insured.

Share Draft Account
A credit union's equivalent of a bank's checking account.

 If you have the opportunity to join a federally insured credit union, you absolutely should.

Credit Union Info
To find a credit union near you, call 800-358-5710.
  To learn how to start one, write:

> *Credit Union National Association*
>   Box 431
>   Madison, WI 57301

Eight Painless Ways to Save, $25 at a Time

Now that you've opened your checking and savings account, you can begin to build your emergency nest egg, that money for a rainy day. You might, of course, win the lottery or clean out a casino, like Dustin Hoffman in the movie *Rain Man*, and then be able to pay off your education loans, buy a house, and live the good life. But don't count on it. Most likely you'll have to take the more conventional and slightly slower route to financial independence.

The rule of thumb: save three, better yet six, months of living expenses; then if you lose your job, become ill, or for some other reason are not working, you have money to tide you over. This nest egg should be in a safe, interest-bearing investment.

Rule of 72
To determine how long it will take to double your money at various interest rates, divide the rate into 72 and you'll get the number of years, assuming interest is compounded annually.

Interest rate	Years to double money
3%	24.0
4%	18.0
5%	14.4
6%	12.0
7%	10.2
8%	9.0
9%	8.0
10%	7.2

---

1. *Treat* your savings like a monthly bill. Put aside money before you spend it. Once a month when you pay your bills, write out a check to deposit in a savings account. Make it the second check you

How Monthly Savings Add Up

Look at what happens if you invest $100 or $300 each month at a fixed rate of 8%, not taking into consideration taxes.

Monthly Amount	Number Of Years			
	5	10	15	20
$100	$ 7,348	$18,295	$ 34,604	$ 58,902
$300	22,043	54,884	103,811	176,706

(Source: Credit Union National Association, Inc.)

write—the first being your rent or mortgage. Begin by saving 1% of your take-home pay the first month and increase the amount by 1% each year. If you can afford it, double or triple the percent you sock away.

2. *Use* an automatic savings plan. It's hard to spend money you never see. Sign up at work; have a set amount taken out of your paycheck and automatically transferred to your bank or credit union savings account or into the firm's thrift plan.

3. *Direct* your bank to regularly transfer a specific sum on a monthly basis from checking into savings or a money market deposit account.

4. *Buy* EE Savings Bonds. Many companies have an automatic plan for purchasing these ultra-safe bonds. Again, you never see the money—it's funneled out of your paycheck. Bonds sell for as little as $25, although your firm may have a slightly higher monthly minimum. (NOTE: You can also purchase bonds at your bank, and there's no fee involved.)

5. *Sign up* for your company's stock purchase plan. These offer employees an opportunity to accumulate stock in the company for which they work, usually through automatic payroll deductions. There are various types of plans—some

even let workers buy the stock at a discount and with no broker's commission.

6. *Save regularly.* Almost every money market mutual fund lets you buy a specified dollar amount of shares at regular intervals if you authorize the fund to take money out of your bank account (see sidebar for funds with low minimum requirements). Sign up by filling in the automatic investment section of a fund's application form and enclosing a bank deposit slip or blank check imprinted with your account number, but first write "void" on the check.

7. *Make* regular payments. After paying off a car loan, college bills, or other debts, continue to write a check for the same dollar amount, or at least half the amount, and stash it in your savings. You've been living without that money each month; now save it. Switching debt for savings is an easy way to stockpile dollars.

8. *Increase* withholding. By taking fewer deductions than you deserve you set aside more money than necessary and guarantee yourself a refund when tax time rolls around. Since you never see the money, it's a painless way to save, although

---

Mini-Savings Plans
These money market funds let you buy shares for $25 or $50/month and will automatically take the money out of your savings or checking account. Sign up with the highest yielding one at the time you call for the forms.

- Twentieth Century Cash Reserve 800-345-2021
- MIM Money Market Fund 800-233-1240
- Berger Money Market Fund 800-333-1001

---

you don't earn interest on these funds. (NOTE: If you are self-employed or a freelancer and want to achieve the same result, pay more than the specified amount on your quarterly estimated tax installments.)

To Have $100,000 At Age 65, Save This Much Each Month

Age You Begin Saving	5%	7%	9%
25	$ 66/month	$ 38/month	$ 21/month
35	$120/month	$ 82/month	$ 55/month
45	$243/month	$192/month	$150/month
55	$643/month	$577/month	$516/month

(Source: Custom Communications)

5 Handling Credit and Credit Cards

In the 1967 movie, *The Graduate*, Dustin Hoffman, who plays a recent college graduate, is told by the father of one of his friends that he should make a career in plastics. The father may not have been referring to plastic credit cards, but perhaps he should have—it's a rapidly growing business.

Credit cards have become so popular that we now live in an almost cashless society. Credit cards are extremely convenient and certainly beat carrying around huge amounts of cash. They have many real key advantages: You get one bill for a number of items; can quickly document business and other expenses; easily purchase items by mail order; take advantage of sale items; use them as proof of identity; make and guarantee hotel, plane, train, cruise, and restaurant reservations; obtain cash advances (especially useful when in a foreign country); rent a car, van, or RV; and build up a good credit rating or history.

The last point is particularly important, for sometime in the future you'll want to borrow a pile of cash—to buy a car, a house, to send your own kids to college, to launch a business—and you certainly can't do this unless you have established a good credit history—meaning that you've paid your bills on time.

So, as long as you use credit cards carefully, you'll benefit from their advantages. But beware of how you use plastic: It's tempting to charge things you want now and pay later over time in periodic installments and at exorbitantly high interest rates. (The average credit card interest rate on unpaid balances is 16.5%). And, now that you're on your own, there's no one (such as parents) to tell you not to. The lending institutions, in fact, will actually encourage you to buy that CD player or new suit that you really can't afford. In one recent year, nearly 900,000 Americans discovered they had purchased one too many CD players and were forced to file for personal bankruptcy. That's a statistic you don't want to join.

The Largest Number of Valid Credit Cards
The collection owned by Walter Cavanaugh of Santa Clara, CA. Known as "Mr. Plastic Fantastic," he has 1,208 different cards. The wallet in which he keeps them weighs 35 pounds.

(Source: Guinness Book of World Records)

Types of Credit Cards

Credit cards are issued by banks, oil companies, retail stores, and travel and entertainment companies, and they have a close cousin, the debit card. Each type of card comes with its own set of terms and conditions.

Bank Credit Cards

These are issued by banks, brokerage firms, and other companies; you know them as Visa or MasterCard. They usually have:

> *Annual fees*: Although there are some no-fee cards, most impose a yearly fee.
>
> *Lines of credit*: This preset dollar figure is the most you can charge; ranges from $500 to $5,000 or more. These can be increased.
>
> *Interest rates on unpaid balances*: Banks can, within broad terms, charge whatever they like and set whatever payment terms they like.
>
> *Cash advances*: These are expensive loans with interest beginning to mount up as soon as the advance is made; most advances also have a high loan fee.

The First Major Credit Card
The first major credit card was launched by Frank McNamara, a businessman who found himself without enough cash to pay for his guests at a New York restaurant. On February 25, 1950, his company issued the first multi-use charge card. Called a Diners Club Card, it had a $5 annual fee, was accepted in just 27 places, and, during that first year, only 200 people carried the card.

Travel and Entertainment Cards

Issued by American Express, Diners Club, and Carte Blanche, these are technically charge cards, not credit cards, and you must pay your bill in full within 20 to 30 days. They are useful when traveling as there are no preset spending limits—airline, train, and cruise tickets along with meals can quickly gobble up the line of credit on a Visa or MasterCard.

Use if you are tempted to run up a balance on your bank credit card.

Premium Cards
These special status cards have higher annual fees than most, higher lines of credit, and certain extras. For example, the American Express gold card.

Debit Cards
Many banks issue MasterCard, Visa, or their own debit cards. These are essentially electronic checkbooks and do not offer credit. Instead of a monthly bill, the bank automatically transfers payment from your checking account as soon as it is notified of your purchase. The advantage is that you don't have to write checks for these charges. And, you're forced to pay your bills at once, so you also avoid incurring high interest rates.

 Use if you need the imposed discipline of not running up credit card debt.

The key disadvantage is that if your checking account earns interest, you lose interest when the money is withdrawn, whereas with a credit card that you pay monthly, your money can be earning interest. An ATM card, when used to get cash, is a debit card, and so are cards that you use at a cash register by tapping in your personal identification number (PIN) into a keypad at the counter.

Secured Credit Cards
People with spotty credit histories or those with no credit history at all once found credit cards very tough to acquire. But as credit card markets reach saturation, some banks are willing to sign up customers who wouldn't have been acceptable before. To get a "se-

cured" card, you must put $250 to $2,000 or more on deposit with the bank and then charge no more than that amount to the card. In other words, you must keep collateral in the issuing institution against possible default that amounts to at least as much money as you can borrow on the card.

Interest rates and annual fees for these cards tend to be high. New applicants often pay steep sign-up fees plus a first-year annual fee. The advantage is that after a year or two with a good payment record, secured card holders can "graduate" to an unsecured card with lower costs.

"In God we trust—all others pay cash."
Sign on an Arkansas diner.

Getting Your First Card

If you've never had your own credit card, or perhaps only used one your parents gave you for emergencies, it will take a little effort on your part to get your own. In fact, you must be prepared for the amount of red tape involved and for possibly receiving several rejections. Yet, even people with good jobs or who have been born with a silver spoon in their mouth sometimes are turned down because they have not established official creditworthiness.

 If you have a credit card with your name on it but it's actually your parent's account, you have *not* established your own credit history. Apply for your own card.

First-time applicants always find it tough to get a credit card, but it's not an impossible hurdle.

If you're in school and one of the companies is on campus luring students to get a card, sign on, but be certain to follow the guidelines below so you won't build up too much debt. When you begin working, you can change to a lower rate card. (Most cards issued to college students have very high rates.)

Steps to take to get a card:

1. Pick a card suited to you. If you intend to pay your credit card bills in full each month, the interest rate makes no difference. So look for a card with no annual fee and a long grace period. For example, a card with a 30-day grace period is giving you a 30-day interest-free loan. If you do not pay your bill in full (but you should aim to), look for a card with a low rate of interest; you'll also probably have to pay a high annual fee. By shopping for the best credit card deal you'll save some money—a few hundred dollars can mean the difference between sweltering in your apartment on summer weekends, or spending them at the beach or the lake.

2. Fill out the application accurately. These are available at individual banks, savings and loans, or by calling an issuer. The application tells potential creditors about your financial history and stability, your income and ability to repay a loan, as well as your assets and liabilities. Answer all questions honestly; do not exaggerate your income. Lies eventually show up in a computer check. Keep a copy of your application.

3. Open checking and savings accounts in your legal name. If you are a woman, that's your first name and either your maiden name or your hus-

band's last name, or a combination of the two: Samantha Taylor Jones, not Mrs. Ralph Jones. If you are single and have a common last name, use a middle initial to avoid confusion with others. Then make regular deposits, no matter how small, into your savings account; these deposits immediately indicate your financial stability.

4. Have utilities listed in your legal name; if you are married, list them in both names. Pay these bills promptly.

5. Apply for a local credit card. Try your neighborhood department store, drugstore, or hardware store. Charge items instead of paying cash and, again, pay your bills promptly. How you repay bills becomes an essential part of your credit history.

    Then, in four to six months . . .

6. Apply for a small loan at your bank, whether you need it or not, and even if it's necessary for you to get someone to cosign. Put the money you borrow into an interest-bearing account at the same bank and make your loan payments when they're due.

 You may have to apply several times before obtaining a card. If you are consistently turned down, read the section "Credit Bureaus" below for additional hints or try for a secured credit card.

Enhancements and freebies are enticing and, depending upon your lifestyle, valuable; but interest rates and fees remain the most important factors in selecting a credit card.

Questions to ask before getting a card:

- What is the interest rate on unpaid balances?
- For how long is this rate guaranteed?
- What is this rate keyed to? (Prime is generally best.)
- Can I switch between a fixed and a variable rate?
- Is there an annual fee? If so, what is it?
- What is the cap on cash advances? What is the interest rate?
- What is the penalty for exceeding the credit limit?
- Is there a late payment charge? How much?
- Is there a lower rate for good customers? Who qualifies?
- How long does this performance-related rate last?
- Does this card have travel-accident insurance, extended warranties, and/or purchase protection, cash rebates?
- Do purchases made qualify for airline frequent flier miles?
- Are there discounts on long distance telephone calls?
- What benefits are offered when card holders are in foreign countries? Legal or medical aid? Overnight replacement of a lost card? Message center? Cash advances?

Passing The Credit Card Course

Whether you already have a card or are just getting one, take your credit card seriously, otherwise you can wind up ruining your credit rating, making it difficult to get a mortgage, education loan, or simply live without debt worries. In addition, a huge debt may limit your career choices, forcing you to opt for a job that you really don't want but one that pays well. And, working primarily to pay off mounds of credit card debt can also sidetrack you from getting more education or learning a new skill.

You Can Leave Home Without Them

Throughout your life you'll be bombarded with seductive appeals from banks, stores, and others to "buy now, pay later." It may seem that having a gold card, a platinum card, or simply any card gives you a lot of clout, prestige, and buying power, but too much plastic can result in runaway debt. Many Americans carry three to eight cards, when two or three would do; the fewer you have, the less temptation to charge items thoughtlessly.

Here's how not to run up credit card debt and to pass the credit card course with flying colors:

- Don't accept new credit cards received in the mail, unsolicited.

- Don't apply for credit cards you don't need.

- To resist impulse buying, leave your credit cards at home unless you have a specific need in mind; then carry only one card.

- Keep credit card receipts; enter them into your financial diary. Because there's no written running balance as in a checkbook, it's easy to lose track of how much you're spending.

- Put a ceiling on your spending. Don't let the credit card company do this for you. They're usually delighted to increase your limit each year and tempt you to spend that much more. Set a monthly limit and stick to it.

- Pay your credit card bill in full at the end of each month.

If you carry a $15,000 balance on your credit card, in just one year, with a 14% interest rate, you'll pay more than $2,100 in interest.

- Spend no more than 20% of your monthly take-home income on credit card debt (excluding mortgage). This is a general guideline; keep it lower if possible and yet realize that at certain times in your life it may be slightly more. This includes car loans and credit card and gasoline card purchases.

Protecting Your Card
- Never add phone numbers and addresses to credit slips, even if merchants request them. Many states have made it illegal to require this information.
- Draw a line through any blank spaces above the total amount on the credit slip so the dollar amount cannot be altered.
- Destroy carbons.

- Better rates are often available at local banks. Some give customers an edge . . . for instance, if you have a checking, savings, or money market account, you may get a no-fee or low percentage interest rate. ASK.
- Check out credit unions. Some give no-fee and/or low fee cards to members who have their monthly paycheck deposited directly into a checking or savings account at the credit union.
- Consider an out-of-state institution with lower rates or no annual fee.

Seven ways to cut credit expenses

1. Pay your credit card bill in full every month and avoid incurring very high interest rates.

2. Use a low interest rate card if you do not pay your bill in full every month.

3. Use a no annual fee card if you pay your bill in full every month.

4. Skip gold or platinum cards (most have hefty annual fees) unless you qualify for a no-fee premium card.

5. Get cash advances only for an emergency; rates are too high and you could dig yourself into a deep hole.

6. If you have piled up debt on several cards, pay off the highest rate card first.

7. Make your loan payments automatically from your checking account; you then may get your credit card loan rate reduced; ASK at your bank or credit union.

Your Credit File

Big Brother, also known as a credit bureau, is keeping track of how you pay your bills. These international computerized organizations are in the business of buying and selling information, and they keep track of any financial missteps you take. When creditors loan money, they want to be reasonably certain they'll be paid back; but since they don't know you personally, they rely on records of how you have handled credit in the past to determine if you are reliable. Credit bureaus, however, do NOT rate consumers; they simply supply the information about your current and previous credit accounts to banks, finance companies, potential employers, insurance companies, and merchants. As paying subscribers, these organizations have access to the credit bureau's files and in return submit their own monthly customer credit account records to the credit bureau.

What's in Your File?

Credit bureaus collect three types of data about you: personal statistics, account information, and facts about your legal record. Personal statistics include your name, past and present addresses, social security number, and employment information that may or may not include your salary and time on the job. Account information consists of detailed data from creditors, including when the account was opened, the credit balance and credit line, number of late payments, and current balance due. Legal information includes things about marriage, divorce, personal bankruptcy, judgments, tax liens, arrests, and convictions.

 Credit bureaus are as crucial a factor in getting a loan or mortgage as your grades and SAT scores were for getting into college. Do not downplay their importance. A negative report could prevent you from getting a job, buying a home or car, or even renting an apartment.

How to Get a Copy of Your Report

Once you have established credit, request a copy of your credit report at least once a year to check for possible errors. Do this whether or not you are trying for a loan—mistakes do happen, and you want your record to be accurate when and if you should need money. A wrong digit in your social security number or letter in your name can put data from someone else's file into yours and turn you into a deadbeat. There are three major credit bureaus, TRW, Equifax, and Trans Union, as well as hundreds of smaller, local ones. Most Americans are in the computers of at least two of the big three. To find out which one is the key network in your area, ask the credit department of a local store or the credit card division of your local bank (see "To Learn More" for their names and telephone numbers). Contact local bureaus by checking in the Yellow Pages under "Credit Bureaus."

Once you have your report you'll have to spend some time sorting it out—it's not in an easy-to-follow format. If you have any difficulty deciphering the data, call the company. Check the footnotes on the back to decipher the symbols; for instance, on TRW reports, "C/OAM" means "charge-off account," indicating that a creditor has written you off as a bad risk for nonpayment.

Fixing Mistakes

If you find an error, photocopy your report, circle the error and correct it, and return it to the agency accompanied by a letter explaining what was wrong. The law requires the agency to act upon your complaint; and if they cannot verify the data in question, it must be removed from your file. If you request, the bureau must then notify any creditor who saw the incorrect information during the past six months.

 If a credit bureau refuses to change your report, the law entitles you to insert a 100-word statement explaining your side of the disputed entry.

Your Rights Under the Fair Credit Reporting Act

You have the right . . .

1. To learn whose report hurt your credit or loan application.
2. To learn the substance of all information except medical, which the agency has on file about you.
3. To find out the sources of this information.

4. To find out who has received your file within the last six months, or within the last year if the report was requested for employment purposes.

5. To get all incorrect data investigated and, if found to be incorrect, deleted from your file.

6. To put into your file a 100-word statement clarifying the facts in remaining disputed information.

7. To have the bureau notify all agencies of the credit bureau's mistake.

8. To have any adverse information erased after 7 years; after 10 if you have declared bankruptcy.

If You're a Credit Card Junkie

Many Americans regard easy credit as a birthright and then wake up to find themselves "another day older and deeper in debt" as Tennessee Ernie Ford crooned in his 1955 hit, "Sixteen Tons." First there was the car, then the vacation at Club Med, followed by too many dinners out.

In fact, no matter how much you earn, at some time in your life you'll probably run into money troubles. If this happens, and I hope it doesn't, there are a number of things you can do to turn life around for the better.

Solving the Problem on Your Own
If the bill collector is at your door, before panicking and calling your favorite aunt for help or taking off for the border, work out a plan and try to get out from under by improving your money habits. Although there are no quick fixes, these 5 steps are a good beginning toward being debt free and having peace of mind.

1. *Get the facts.* Begin by filling in the worksheet below to determine how much you really owe.

2. *Set up and follow a bare-bones budget.*

3. *Make minimum monthly payments* on all your bills and then begin paying off higher interest rate cards first, based on the information in your worksheet.

4. *Don't hide.* Running away from your creditors will only ruin your credit history. Instead, write to each one (in the case of Visa or MasterCard, contact the issuing bank) and explain the situation, suggesting the amount you can pay monthly. Be realistic. Keep a copy of your letter—it notifies creditors of your sincere willingness to meet your obligations. Most are flexible and will work out a re-payment plan you can handle. And, they're not dumb—they'd rather extend your loan term or reduce the size of your payments than get zero from you.

5. *Consolidate your house of cards.* Discuss combining all loans into one giant one with a lower rate of interest. Discuss this with your bank. If you can reduce your loan interest rate by at least 2%, it's generally worthwhile. But remember, it will be successful *ONLY* if you close your old charge accounts and tear up those cards.

Average Credit Card Debt
The typical CCCS client owes $19,600 to at least ten different creditors. It takes them an average of 44 months to pay off all lenders.

Getting Professional Help

If you can't clean up your debts on your own, then it's time to get outside help. Banks and credit unions often give debt counseling to customers. Or, if you're seriously in debt, use a reputable nonprofit credit counseling service. To locate the one nearest you, call the National Foundation for Consumer Credit, 800-388-2227, the umbrella organization for some 500+ local Consumer Credit Counseling Services nationwide. These nonprofit services offer free or low-cost help for getting out of debt, reestablishing your creditworthiness, and teaching you how to handle your money. They may ask you to surrender all credit cards and operate with cash only. They often negotiate with your creditors to lower an interest payment, stretch out a loan, or set up a long-term payment plan that is acceptable.

Are You Headed For Trouble?

1. Do you borrow for things you used to buy with cash?
2. Does more and more of your income go to pay off debts?
3. Are you borrowing to pay for food and/or rent?
4. Are you at or very near the limit on your lines of credit?
5. Are you uncertain about how much you owe?
6. Can you only pay the minimum amount due on your credit cards?
7. Are you taking out new loans or new credit cards before paying off old loans?
8. Are your monthly credit payments more than 20% of your net income, minus rent or mortgage?

If you answered yes to two of these questions, stop using your credit cards immediately and begin paying off your loans, even if it's only a few dollars a week. If you answered yes to number 5, fill in the worksheet below.

Software Help
To determine how much you'll save by making regular extra monthly payments on your credit card debt and other tips reducing what you owe, try easy-to-use "The Banker's Secret Credit Card" software; $28 including shipping, 800-255-0899.

Avoid private "credit repair" centers. Fees are often very hefty and the advertised credit "fix" is typically not real or even possible.

Your Credit Picture At A Glance

Name of creditor	Date of last payment	Total due/ credit line	Interest rate	Monthly payment	Date due

This worksheet will give you a quick picture of your credit obligations. List all consumer debts and loans. Total the monthly amount due and then figure out the percentage of your take-home pay that it represents. If it's higher than 20%, you're headed for trouble. And, ask yourself: Can I pay off all these debts, except a mortgage, within 18 to 24 months? If the answer is no, you're in over your head.

Cardinal Credit Card Rules For Couples

Credit's a pretty easy issue if it only involves you. But if you're living with someone or married, complications often crop up. When you team up with someone else, it's important to play your credit cards right in order to preserve your own creditworthiness.

For Live-Togethers
Separate credit cards are best for singles living together.

If you give your live-in partner authorization to use your credit card and you break up and he or she continues to run up bills and not pay them, you are NOT protected legally. You can cancel the authorization, but you still are responsible for the bills. (If you were married, you could make the debt a factor in the divorce negotiations.)

 Live-togethers do have legal protection in one instance: if you both sign a loan agreement. Then you can sue if your friend does not pay his/her share, but this can be expensive and unpleasant.

For Marrieds
Keep your own credit history.

Putting all credit obligations in one spouse's name may seem convenient, but it leaves the other one without a credit history in the event of divorce or death. Then the odds are that credit applications by the one without a credit record will be denied because he or she will not have a sufficient track record of how debts were paid to stores, banks, and others.

Solution: Keep at least one charge card in your own name so both of you can get credit when you need it.

Most bank cards offer individual accounts with authorized "secondary users." Being a secondary user does not carry much weight; make certain you are a primary card holder.

To Learn More

The best credit cards are often unadvertised. To find the best ones, contact:

• *Credit Card Locator* ($19)

Consumer Credit Card Rating Service
    P.O. Box 5483
    Oxnard, CA 93031
    310-392-7720
    Annual fees, interest rates, and other info on 1,000 credit cards arranged by state; handy wheel helps you factor different spending and payment habits into a card's annual cost.

• *Bankcard Holders of America*

560 Herndon Parkway
    Suite 120
    Herndon, VA 22070
    800-553-8025; 703-481-1110
    Separate lists of bank cards with low interest rates, with no annual fees, and recommended secured cards, @ $4. Pamphlet, "How To Choose a Credit Card," $1.00.

To get a copy of your credit file, contact:

TRW Credit Data
  Box 2350
  Chatsworth, CA 91313-2350
  800-392-1122; 214-235-1200

Equifax Credit Information Services
  Box 740241
  Atlanta, GA 30374
  800-685-1111

Trans Union Corporation
  Box 7000
  North Olmsted, OH 44070
  312-408-1050

6 Borrowing and Lending Money

Neither a borrower, nor a lender be, For loan oft loses both itself and friend.

Hamlet, Act I, scene 3

Shakespeare

We'd all do well to heed this advice that Polonius gave to his son, Laertes, as he headed off for school. Nevertheless, there will be times in your life when it is necessary, even wise, to borrow money—to pay for school, to buy a house, co-op, condo, or car, or perhaps to start a business. In this chapter we'll look at how to handle loans between friends and with members of your family as well as those from other sources—banks, credit unions, life insurance policies, even from your pension fund. Armed with the facts, you'll be able to get the best terms and avoid taking on too much debt.

A Loan Between Friends and Relatives

If You're the Lender
Although it's a well-known fact that finances and friendship seldom mix, and that loans between friends have a high default risk, it's also true that turning away a friend in need is very difficult, sometimes impossible,

particularly if the request is for a legitimate reason, such as for a security deposit on an apartment, to visit or care for an ailing parent, or to make ends meet after losing a job. If you decide to make a friendly loan, be sensible and protect yourself by lending only an amount that you can afford to lose. And before making the loan, ask yourself:

- Will I need that $500 or $5,000 if I have an emergency? Do I have enough in my savings account to meet an unexpected expenditure?
- Is my friend reliable? Will he/she meet payment deadlines?
- Is he/she too heavily in debt for me to really be helpful?
- Has my friend tried to get a bank loan and been turned down? (If so, assess that information. Being the lender of last resort is not a wise position in which to be.)
- Will I mind the change in the balance of power in our relationship? (The borrower always loses some self-esteem and the lender, gaining the upper hand, often becomes critical of the friend's spending habits.)

A loan need not necessarily rupture a relationship, however, and if you decide to go ahead, your chances of not losing the loan or your friend will be enhanced if you handle the transaction in a businesslike manner. You are not doing either of you a favor by merely saying, "Just pay me back whenever you can."

"A verbal contract isn't worth the paper it's printed on."—Sam Goldwyn, founder of MGM

Instead, set up a formal, written plan, including the amount of the loan, a repayment schedule, and the interest rate, just as a banker would. You can use a promissory note, available at stationery stores.

Interest
Cost of borrowing money, stated as a percentage rate.

Be certain to charge interest—the prime rate is a good benchmark and yet is typically lower than bank loan rates, which will help your friend save money. You both should sign and date the document. Keep a copy: If it turns into a bad debt, it may be tax deductible as a short-term capital loss in the year in which the debt became worthless.

Prime Rate
The interest rate a bank charges its top-rated commercial borrowers.

However, you must have proof, both that the debt was not collectible and not a gift. Good records and interest payments help differentiate between a gift and a loan in the eyes of the IRS.

 If the loan is for $10,000 or more, interest earned is taxed as income to the lender. Talk to your accountant about the tax implications of loans this size or larger.

If your friend misses a payment, address the issue right away by writing a note or calling. Ask if there's a problem, or you may want to tell him/her you have some expenses and could use the money. If he/she never makes any payments, you can try to collect in small claims court for a nominal fee. If that doesn't work, simply chalk it up to experience and never repeat your mistake.

If You're the Borrower
Approaching a friend or family member for money can be awkward, but if you need the money for a truly serious and important reason (and for only a short time), doing so will be less difficult. Before asking, be certain that your friend or relative can easily afford to lend you the money and that you will indeed be able to pay it back. It's best not to ask for money at a social or family gathering; instead arrange for an appointment to discuss your financial need. At that time indicate not only how much you need to borrow, but why, for how long, that you will pay interest, and where you will get the money to pay back the loan.

How to Say "No"
If you don't want to loan someone money, you can still be helpful by giving your friend or relative a small financial gift, making it clear that this is all you are willing to do. Or, if you sense that no amount of money will remedy the situation and will at best temporarily plug a financial hole, put your friend in touch with a bank that might be able to grant a loan or offer to pay for a session with a financial planner who will set up a working budget.

Dealing with a Freeloader or Sponge
Every once in a while you will run into someone who constantly taps friends or co-workers for infusions of money—five dollars here, ten dollars there—often for bus fare or to pay for a taxi or lunch.

And, it seems as though this type of person conveniently forgets that he owes others money. Don't be

> "Creditors have better memories than debtors."—Ben Franklin, *The Way to Wealth*.

foolish and keep feeding into this bottomless pit. You can politely deter such requests by firmly saying, "I'd like to help you out, but you still owe me $5."

Cosigning a Loan

If you're asked to cosign a loan by a friend or relative, think carefully: Should you put your credit rating in the hands of someone who cannot get money on their own? And, can you afford to lose the money—should it come to that? Sometimes, of course, cosigning makes good sense—to help a friend or relative get credit for the first time, for example.

When you cosign, you are not merely vouching for the borrower's character—YOU ARE ASSUMING FULL LIABILITY FOR THE LOAN IF THE BORROWER DOES NOT PAY IT BACK. And, this liability includes late fees and collection costs. Lenders may also seek money from the cosigner without first going after the borrower, and lenders may also sue the cosigner.

If your significant other, for instance, asks you to cosign a car loan, consider what you'll do if that person does not meet the monthly payments and the finance company demands that you pay off the debt. You may not even know that your friend is behind in making payments until you receive a letter from the lender demanding that you come up with the back payments. By that point, the lender may have reported you (as well as your friend) to a credit bureau, thus damaging your credit history. The matter could become more complicated and painful if your friend becomes your ex-friend.

 To avoid such unpleasant surprises, ask the bank to put in writing that it will notify you at once of any late or missed payments.

Secured Loan
One that is backed or secured by something tangible—real estate, a car, savings accounts, securities.

Types of Commercial Loans

There are several basic types of commercial or non-personal loans: secured, unsecured, automatic overdrafts, and lines of credit; but there are just two ways they are repaid: by installments (regular monthly payments) or by a single payment—also known as a term loan and repaid in a lump sum at the end of the loan period.

Unsecured Loan
One that is not backed by a tangible asset; also known as a signature loan. Credit card loans are unsecured.

Before you take out any type of loan, ask yourself if you *really* need to borrow the money; if you can use your savings instead, and if the loan will bury you in too much debt.

Banks, credit unions, even brokerage firms are all in the business of selling cash. To find the best deal, study the information below, conquer the jargon, and follow steps 1 through 4. Remember, the shorter the loan length, the higher the monthly payments but the lower the total finance charge.

1. *Call your bank first.* Banks and credit unions often give lower rates or faster approval for their own customers. Then . . .
2. *Comparison shop.* Rates and terms vary widely, even among banks in the same town. Set aside some telephone time to gather the facts.
3. *Go for a secured loan first.* If you put up collateral, the interest rate will be lower than with an unsecured loan based merely on your signature.

Collateral
The property or assets pledged as security for a loan, such as a savings account, CD, securities, or real estate. If the borrower defaults, the lender can sell the collateral and use the proceeds to satisfy the remaining debt.

---

4. *Track interest rates.* Many loan rates are adjustable, moving up and down with the Treasury bill rate, the prime rate, or some other official rate. If you take out an adjustable loan, make certain you can handle any increase in rates.

Adjustable Rate Loan
One whose interest rate fluctuates with a key rate, such as the rate paid on Treasury bills; opposite of fixed rate.

Secured Personal Loans

Banks will lend money using your savings account or CD as collateral, charging 2 to 4% more than the rate they are paying on these very same deposits. If you fail to pay off your loan, the bank will deduct both the principal and interest from your deposit.

 If you're self-disciplined, skip the loan and withdraw money from your savings account and pay it back as soon as possible—in effect, borrow from yourself. Don't cash in a CD before maturity, however, because you'll be slapped with a penalty.

Unsecured Loans

If you don't have collateral, you may still be able to get a bank loan, but you'll have to pay a higher interest rate. Unsecured lines of credit at banks and credit unions allow you access to from $2,000 to $25,000 by writing a check. The amount you qualify for depends on your income and credit rating. Most such loans have a fixed rate of interest with three years to repay. Late-payment penalties and annual fees can be high.

 Some banks offer good clients a lower rate if you maintain a sizable deposit in your checking account. ASK.

Credit Card Loans

You can tap a line of credit on your Visa, MasterCard, or most any other bank card by simply writing a check.

 These are extremely seductive and should only be used in an emergency until you can negotiate a better deal elsewhere.

Secured Credit Card Loans

A growing number of banks offer a secured Visa or MasterCard. Your credit line is based on the amount of deposit you have in the bank. The bank can tap your deposits if your payments are overdue.

Use only a bank that pays interest on your deposits.

> **Equity**
> The amount of property you own outright; it's based on the fair market value minus any outstanding principal due (on your mortgage in the case of real estate).

Home Equity Loans

Because interest on consumer loans (those just described) is not tax deductible and interest on home equity loans generally is, it may make sense to use your house or co-op as a way to borrow, but ONLY FOR IMPORTANT PURPOSES. There are two types of such loans: the old-fashioned "second mortgage" or closed-end loan, in which you borrow a fixed amount all at once and repay it in monthly installments over a set period, such as ten years; and the newer home equity line of credit, through which you borrow money as you need it against a maximum established when you open the account. You pay interest on the balance due, just as with a credit card. Most lenders will give you 70 to 80% of the appraised value of the house, minus what you owe on it. The amount also depends upon your income, but the typical minimum line of credit is $10,000. Loan periods vary all over the lot—from two or five years to twenty, and during that time you tap into the account by writing checks or using a special credit card. With this type of loan you borrow only when you need the money, and you are not required to fill out additional loan applications— only the initial one. Rates tend to be lower than other lines of credit because the loan is secured by the equity in your house.

A 1% boost on a $100,000, 30-year loan increases the monthly payment by $78 and winds up costing $28,080 more.

 Use only for major expenditures, such as education, an automobile, and home improvements. DO NOT USE for vacations or luxuries—if you do, you could find yourself quickly and deeply in debt, and if you're unable to make your payments, the bank can repossess your house.

In 1824, when Charles Dickens was 12 years old, his father owed money to several merchants. Although his house was not repossessed, he went where most debtors did back then: to prison. After three months, his family and friends paid the bills and he was released. They never charged him interest.

Principal
The balance of a debt.

Other Sources of Loans

IRA's
You can withdraw money from each IRA for 60 days once a year with no penalty and with no interest charges.

 If the money is not put back into your account within the 60 days, you must pay taxes plus a 10% penalty on the amount outstanding.

If you have two IRAs, stagger borrowing in order to have access to the cash for 120 days, but think twice before borrowing from your retirement kitty. It should be a last resort because in reality you're robbing yourself to pay Paul, taking away future income from your own retirement nest egg.

Retirement Accounts

Many companies allow employees to borrow from the 401(k) or other qualified plans. Loans are limited to the greater of $10,000 or half the vested balance, up to $50,000. You must pay the debt back in five years, although if it's to purchase a primary residence, you may be given longer.

Vested
The amount an employee has a right to receive from the benefits contributed by an employer to a pension, profit-sharing, stock purchase, or other plan. The length of time it takes to become fully vested varies.

 If you do not pay back your loan, the outstanding principal is subject to taxes plus a 10% penalty. Repayment is usually through payroll withholding. With most 401(k) plans, if you leave your job with a loan outstanding, you must repay it immediately.

 Although the interest is not tax deductible on these loans, it does go back into your account, not to the bank. This interest can then accumulate additional earnings that are tax-deferred until you withdraw them.

Life Insurance

Policyholders can borrow against the cash value of a universal or whole life policy with no questions asked. Usually you can repay the loan whenever you like, but remember you bought the insurance to protect your family in the event of your death, and any amount of loan outstanding when you die will be deducted from the money slated to go to your beneficiaries.

Cash Value
The dollar amount you may borrow against a life insurance policy. Part of your insurance payments or premiums buy death benefits and part go into an investment account that pays either fixed or variable rates of return . . . it's the latter that can be borrowed. This amount grows over time as dividends, interest, and premiums accumulate.

 While the interest on the loan is not tax deductible, it is paid back into your own plan and accumulates tax-deferred until withdrawn.

Getting a Loan
If you're headed back to school, chances are you'll need a helping hand. One of the best sources for information is *Don't Miss Out; the Ambitious Student's Guide to Financial Aid* by Robert Leider and Anna Leider, now in the 18th edition. It covers sources of aid for graduate and undergraduate students. $7 from: Octameron Press, Box 2748, Alexandria, VA 22301; 703-836-5480.

Borrowing Money Confidentially

There may be a time in your life when you need money for something you don't want to tell the world about—for a sensitive medical procedure, cosmetic surgery, to help a friend who has asked for privacy, or some other issue. Here are five ways to go about it.

1. *Extended medical payment plan.* Many doctors will allow patients at least 90 days to pay for an expensive medical procedure—even longer. Some may extend payment to six months without interest, provided you set up a plan in advance to make regular payments. Put the details in writing, giving a copy to the physician and keeping one for your files.

2. *Bank loan.* If you have an overdraft checking account at your bank or credit union, you can readily borrow without getting advance approval. Simply sign your name on a check.

3. *Life insurance loan.* If you have a universal or whole life policy, you can borrow from its "cash value," —your built-up savings—generally at low rates. You're really tapping into your own savings, so no disclosure of purpose is required.

4. *Credit card advance.* Use this as a last resort, because you'll be paying sky-high interest rates.

5. *Family and friends.* You may be able to appeal to someone you know well for help without revealing why you need the money (see above).

You, Your Parents and Your Money

Once you're on your own and supporting yourself, you don't want to have your parents meddling in your finances. Even if you wind up making some mistakes, and everyone does, you'd rather call the shots. So-called "helpful" parental advice may not really be all that helpful. On the other hand, you may have parents or other relatives who are extremely wise about money management, and you might do very well to listen to their wisdom. In fact, it could be very foolish on your part to overlook such in-house resources.

If you are fortunate enough to be living in this kind of family, you should approach your Dad or Aunt in a businesslike fashion, asking them to set aside some time to discuss money matters on a regular basis. If you establish a professional tone, in all likelihood they will offer useful suggestions but not intrude.

On the other hand, if your family is meddlesome, then you must learn how to steer clear of volatile topics. Be smart. Don't walk into fights. Use your head. Think in advance. If your Mother believes buying designer suits is extravagant, don't wear your new Armani to Sunday dinner. If your Dad disapproves of spending money on a club membership, don't talk about your golf or tennis game all the time. On the other hand, it is your money, you've earned it and the right to spend it as you see fit, but knowingly aggravating others is not your right, in fact it's not very kind.

To avoid any conflicts and at the same time maintain your financial independence, here are some tips:

- If you and your parents have differing attitudes about money and lifestyles, avoid bringing up your salary, your raise, the amount of your rent or monthly mortgage payment. If they don't know

how much you make or how you're spending it, it
will be tough to fight over it.

- If they ask you questions you prefer not to answer,
simply say, "I appreciate your interest, but I'm
really trying to take care of myself, and so far it's
working well. If I run into a problem, I'll certainly
come to you for advice."

- Consider why your parents hold certain money
attitudes. Perhaps they had to work a long time to
become financially comfortable; perhaps they're
not comfortable even now. If your parents are
divorced, one or the other may have a cash flow
problem. Or, maybe one or both of them has/have
made or inherited a lot of money and they don't
want you to be a spoiled rich kid. Although your
family's financial heritage cannot be altered, it
may help you to understand it, so you can incor-
porate its positive aspects into your life and elimi-
nate the negative ones.

- If your parents give or lend you money, it is almost
axiomatic that they will want you to use it in a
certain way. Few parents make sizable loans or
gifts without strings attached. If they lend you
money for a down payment on a house, to help
cover the expense of having a baby, for graduate
school tuition, or to start up your own business, it
is unreasonable for you to expect them (1) not to
want to be repaid, and (2) not to want to know
that the money is being used for the stated purpose. If you can't stand this, then don't accept the
money.

- If your parents give you money for your birthday,
a holiday, graduation, or wedding anniversary,
they may very well say what it's for. Unless you
really can't use or enjoy what they have in mind,
buy what they intended. On the other hand, if you

feel VERY strongly about using their gift money for something else, you can say, "Mom, if it's alright with you, instead of buying a bond, I'd like to use your gift toward some dishes." If this backfires, you'll have to decide which you prefer: peace between you and your Mom and no new dishes (at least right away), or new dishes but a mother who doesn't want to eat off of them. Remember, this is not a life and death situation for either of you.

- And, be a little patient; the older you get, the more established you become, the less parents tend to meddle.
- Finally, keep all this in mind when you raise your own children.

Your Financial Philosophy

As you move on with your education, career, and family life you'll encounter various financial problems—not only about how to make money, but how to best handle it in a social sense. You will need to evolve some principles for making your financial relationships work smoothly and for enjoying life. Sometimes you'll have to say no, sometimes yes, sometimes a compromise is called for. A friend may ask you to donate a sizable amount to a political campaign; you may be asked to invest in a friend's start-up company, or to join a group for lunch or dinner that spends more than you. A few thoughts on saying yes or no.

- Don't be petty. Some people "nickel and dime" life to death. If you're sharing lunch or dinner with friends, divide the check and forget the fact your meal was $1.85 less than your friend's. If the restaurant is too expensive for your budget, then simply don't go next time you're asked, or suggest a less expensive place to dine.

- Life costs. You can't avoid certain expenses; they are part of life—whether it's earning a living or taking a vacation. If at work the custom is to collect money for wedding and birthday gifts, give something; don't be a scrooge. On the other hand, you are under no obligation ever to give more than you can afford.

- Learn how to say "no" gracefully. If you simply cannot participate when asked to donate money to a cause, then simply say, "I'd really love to, but this comes at a time when my taxes/tuition/mortgage is due." Or, "I'm rather short, but perhaps next time."

- When traveling or dining out, tipping is simply part of the scene, so include it in your budget. Taxi drivers, waiters, doormen, and skycaps all depend upon tips for a living. So do barbers, hairdressers, building supers, shoeshine people, and babysitters.

Getting Off the Couch

Many single people put off making financial decisions such as investing, buying a car, making a down payment on a house, or furnishing an apartment beyond the Salvation Army look. Take care that you don't live like you're camping out. Paint your living room, hang your prints, get a coffee table. Learn to cook for yourself and others. Don't live a postponed life—if you do, you'll overlook investment and professional opportunities. You'll never take that vacation, celebrate the holidays, get back to school, go for a new position. Life is not much fun if it has a temporary quality—as though you're waiting for the right person to come along to live with or to marry. You ARE the right person, and no one will refuse to be your friend, live with you, or marry you because you're financially savvy, because you know how to take care of yourself, because you already own a car, Cuisinart and co-op. Your philosophy should not only be "carpe diem" (seize the day), but seize the financial reins as well.

Handling a Trust Fund

If you are lucky enough to have a trust fund that generates income, you will need to discuss with whoever set up the fund—most likely parents or grandparents—how this money is to be used. Trust funds come in all shapes and sizes, and with various restrictions. Most are established with the intention that the money be used for a child's college education.

You may or may not have the legal right to the money at this point in your life. With some trusts only the interest can be tapped; with others the money is given to the beneficiary at various stages—perhaps some at age 21, more at age 25 or 30.

To avoid running into problems with your trust fund, discuss with your parents how the money should be used. Respect the fact that it is there, but don't ever let it control your life. If you depend solely on the trust for income, you run the risk of always being a kid, of never growing up, and ultimately circumventing the more important task of taking care of yourself, of making your own living. Some people also brag about their trust fund or their family's money. Resist the temptation. You want people to like you for you, not for the fact that someone else in your family saw to it you had a little extra financial backing.

On the other hand, if you use the money carefully and wisely, it will be a reassuring factor in your life, not a controlling one. It may enable you to concentrate on your studies, fund a special project, start your own business, see to it that your children will be able to go to college. It may also empower you to buy a house, travel, become a volunteer, switch careers, take some time off to paint or write the great American novel.

Regardless of the amount of money involved, think of your trust fund, not as a means for living a wild and reckless life, but rather as a wonderful financial cushion, giving you the freedom to develop your potential to the fullest.

And also, regardless of how big or small it is, remember now and then to thank the person that set aside and contributed this money on your behalf, without whom there would be no trust fund.

Enjoying a Windfall

Chances of winning the jackpot on *Wheel of Fortune* or the state lottery are slim, but sometime you may just come into a windfall. You may inherit money, receive a sizable gift or bequest, win a prize, get a bonus at work, receive an insurance settlement. What to do? First write a thank-you note to the giver—your boss, your relative, or, if the giver left you the money in his or her will, to the family of the deceased or to the executor of the will; to the lawyer that won the settlement for you.

Then, put the money in a safe, liquid place, turning a deaf ear to any high-pressured sales pitches. If you haven't written a will, now you should. Review those financial goals you drew up when you read the Introduction to this book and decide how your windfall can help you meet those goals. And, finally, use part of this "free" money to do something special. If you've received money from a grandparent, for example, take a fraction of it and purchase something with lasting value that will always remind you of this loving person. If the money is from an impersonal source, such as a bonus, invest most of it and then take a vacation, buy a new suit, or treat your parents or significant other to a night on the town—after all, money is to be enjoyed as well as saved.

If the amount you receive is too large for you to handle, you'll need professional advice.

Those Old College Loans

Lots of students rack up $15,000 worth of debt long before landing their first job. If they're law or medical school grads, it can be as much as $50,000 to $100,000. Chances are you're among this group.

Go for the Carrot

Repaying your loan on time has its own rewards. If you have a Stafford loan [owned and serviced by the Student Loan Marketing Association (Sallie Mae)], you can get 2% shaved off the interest rate if you make each of the first 48 payments on time through the "Great Rewards" program. Borrowers with a perfect on-time record automatically receive the reduction, although an occasional late payment after the four years won't jeopardize the discount.

The monthly savings may not be huge, but they can add up. For example, if you borrow a total of $5,000, you will save about $250 over the life of the loan; if you borrow $20,000 over 10 years, you will save an average of about $13 a month once the benefit kicks in, for a total of about $985. On a total loan of $23,000, you would save more than $1,100.

Stafford loans have a limit of $23,000 for under-grads and $65,000 for grad students (including under-graduate borrowing). For new borrowers, Stafford loans have variable interest rates that are adjusted annually; the current rate is pegged to the 91-day Treasury bill and has a lifetime cap of 9%. About 900 financial institutions offer the rate reduction program.

Loan Consolidation

Most students wind up with more than just one loan, all with different provisions and interest rates. If this is you, you may want to consolidate your loans. Under a federal program available through lenders, school loans totaling $7,500 or more can be combined so you pay only one monthly check. Under these circumstances, the typical 10-year repayment period can be extended to 20 or even 30 years, which, of course, reduces your monthly payments.

Consolidation, however, has its own price tag. Over the life of the loan you almost inevitably will pay more in interest charges, largely because of extending the loan and to some extent because the 9% minimum interest rate charged consolidated loans may be higher than the initial low rate.

If you are repaying a $9,000 loan at 8%, your monthly payments would be $109. If the loan were consolidated at 9% for a 15-year term, your payments could drop as low as $67.50 for the first two years. Then they would increase to $114.30 a month for the rest of the loan.

But think about interest payments. In this example, without loan consolidation you wind up paying $13,080 in principal and interest over 10 years. If you opt for loan consolidation, the total amount paid over the 15 years would be $19,450.80.

You can apply for loan consolidation from your lending institution or at a bank that participates in the program.

Avoid Defaulting at All Costs

Life is getting tougher for those who default on their student loans. Defaulters are being reported by the Department of Education to the leading credit reporting services—TRW, Equifax, and Trans Union. This should give you incentive to pay.

Loan Lingo

- **Deferment.** Postpones repayment and can stop interest rate meter on some loans.
- **Forbearance.** Postpones repayment of principal but interest rate meter continues running; granted for hardship cases.
- **Consolidation.** Allows you to combine student loans adding up to at least $7,500 or more into one loan. Can often extend length of loan to as many as 30 years; minimum interest rate is 9%.
- **Graduated payment.** Monthly payments in the first years out of school are smaller; they get larger as your annual income rises.

If You Can't Pay

If you don't have a job but are really actively looking, you may be eligible for a deferment. The government grants deferments on its loans for several reasons, including returning to school, being pregnant if recently out of school, being temporarily disabled, or serving in the military.

If you're working but you can't make ends meet, you probably won't qualify for a deferment, but you may be entitled to a forbearance, in which case your principal payments will be suspended but the interest will continue to accrue.

Sometimes you can actually get certain loans forgiven if you teach in a particular area or go into the military.

Although with many loans there's a six-month grace period after graduation before you must start paying, it's best to contact your lender as soon as you sense a problem. Lenders really have quite a lot of flexibility if they believe you intend to repay your loan.

Prepaying Your Loan

Standard loan payments are split between interest and principal, and any amount you prepay is subtracted directly from the principal. That means prepaying has a cumulative effect: It reduces your principal, leaving a smaller balance on which interest can be calculated or charged, so that with each passing month more of your payment goes toward the principal. Even a small amount prepaid each month is worth it.

If instead of prepaying your student loan you save the money, you could be better off, depending upon how much your money earns in the savings account. The hitch is that you must save the money every single week. Will you really do that?

Prepaying Student Loan Versus Saving

Terms:

10 years
9% interest rate on loan
5 ¼% interest on savings
$5,000 loan

Extra $ amount paid per month	Amount saved by prepaying	Amount saved in savings account
$10	$ 572.21	$1,563.48
20	933.12	3,126.96
30	1,182.50	4,690.45
40	1,365.70	6,253.93
50	1,506.15	7,817.41

If You're Married

You're sharing closet space, now you can share your student loans. Married couples can jointly consolidate their student loans into one new account and lower monthly payments by as much as 40%, extend their repayment term, and possibly select a graduated repayment schedule. For details, call: Sallie Mae, 800-524-9100 or 800-643-0040.

7 Simple, Speedy Solutions for Small Savers

You, too, should follow this advice from the founder of McDonald's when it comes to saving. The simpler it is the more likely you'll stash money away—for a vacation, car, house, graduate school.

You're so busy looking for a job or working to keep one that you have no time left over to manage your money. Or maybe you've taken on a new apartment, acquired a new friend, or moved across the country. There are many reasons why all of us, at various times in our lives, neglect our investments. Here's a speed guide to the best places for your savings ... you should aim to have a savings nest egg equal to six months' living expenses before you plunge into the stock market or other arenas. Although it's tempting to simply leave your nest egg in your savings account, don't—the interest rate is way too low. And don't let feelings of laziness or intimidation about financial matters sidetrack you from getting a higher rate. We've made it easy for you—below are seven alternatives.

> **EE Savings Bonds**
> "U.S. Savings Bonds" (free) from:
>
> *Bureau of Public Debt*
> 1300 C Street SW
> Washington, DC 20239

EE Savings Bonds

Sold by the U.S. government to individuals, Series EE Savings Bonds are one of the least expensive, yet safest investments around. The current minimum interest rate for EE bonds held five years is 4%. This rate is adjusted every six months, in May and November, by the U.S. Treasury, based on the average market yield of five-year Treasury notes for the previous six months. EE bonds pay 85% of that market average.

EE bonds not only offer a variable return that can help you keep pace with inflation and rising interest rates, they also provide a modest tax break. You never have to pay state or local taxes on the interest the bonds earn, and federal income tax may be deferred until you cash them in or they mature. When your bonds do mature, you can roll them over into Series HH Savings Bonds and defer taxes even longer.

With savings bonds you won't have to worry about reinvesting your earned interest. In fact, they do not pay current interest but instead are purchased at half their face value and are redeemed at maturity at full face value. In other words, the difference between the price you pay for the bond and the redemption value constitutes your interest.

To buy:
Call 800-US-BONDS for the current interest rate. Bonds are sold at a 50% discount from face value, so a

$50 bond actually costs only $25; a $100 bond is $50. You can buy them at your local bank or through a payroll savings plan where you work. There is no fee for buying or selling these bonds.

Certificates Of Deposit (CDs)

If you have an extra $500 in your savings or checking account that you know you won't be needing for six months or a year, take a look at CDs. They are a better choice in this case than EE Savings Bonds, which cannot be redeemed during the first six months.

Top Yielding CDs
To find the best rates in the nation, check current issues of:

Your Money Magazine

Money Magazine

Barron's (weekly newspaper)

The Wall Street Journal on Wednesday

CDs are a type of time deposit—a specified dollar amount is deposited for a specified period of time. Basically you are lending the bank money for which you will receive interest. The time length of the deposit is determined prior to purchase. CDs run from a few months to several years. Minimums can be anywhere from $100 on up to $100,000.

You must decide how long you want to tie up your money for. The longer the maturity date, the greater the interest rate and the greater the interest rate risk, that is, if rates move up and your money is locked in at the old lower rate. If rates move up, you can cash in your CD, but most banks impose an interest penalty for early redemption. So it's best to buy a CD only if you know you won't need to tap that money prior to maturity.

To buy:
Call three or four banks in your area for current rates, and check one of the financial publications for the nation's highest yielding CDs, such as the Wednesday edition of *The Wall Street Journal.*

Money Market Mutual Funds

If you want immediate access to your money, there are two easy places to invest: a money market mutual fund or a money market deposit at your bank. The funds pay higher rates, so we'll discuss those first. They usually offer about the highest rates possible in an investment that is instantly liquid and very safe.

Money Market Funds With Low Minimums
- MIM Funds, 800-233-1240
- Berger Funds, 800-333-1001
- Twentieth Century, 800-345-2021

Money market mutual funds are investment companies that pool your money with that of other investors and invest it in short-term financial instruments, including high-quality commercial paper, jumbo bank CDs, and government agency debt instruments. The funds are called short term because their securities usually mature in 30 to 90 days. Because of their high-quality portfolios, there's no serious danger that you'll lose your principal or that the fund won't pay interest.

Interest rates vary daily. You receive a monthly statement telling what your investment is worth, what the monthly average return was, and your total dollar investment. Rates for many of the funds are also listed in the newspaper. Your dividends can be automatically reinvested in new shares. You can add to your account or withdraw money at any time without charge.

Most funds also offer check-writing privileges, usually with a minimum of $250 or $500 per check.

 Use your money market fund to pay larger bills and leave only the minimum required in your bank's no- or low-interest rate checking account for paying smaller bills.

To buy:

You can buy money market funds by calling the fund's 800 number. Or, if you have a stockbroker, you can establish a money market fund at the brokerage firm. Keep in mind that shares are set at $1 each, so $1,000 will buy 1,000 shares. Interest is also paid in shares, so the value of a share does not increase. Instead, you will have more shares in your account over time.

Bank Money Market Accounts

Although rates are somewhat lower than money market mutual funds, the ease of opening an account at a familiar bank may lure you in this direction. Do so, especially if your alternative is to do nothing. The key differences between a bank money market account and a money market mutual fund are:

- In a bank money market account, if your account falls below a preset minimum (often $2,000 or

$2,500), the interest rate generally will drop to the passbook rate, or some other lower rate.

- Bank funds are federally insured up to $100,000 per depositor per bank.
- Banks have tougher rules about check writing and automatic transfers. Typically, you cannot make more than six such transactions in one month, with no more than three of these by check. If you exceed these limits, you will be charged a fee. Some banks may even close your account if you consistently exceed the transaction maximums. Money market mutual funds, on the other hand, generally permit unlimited check writing.

To buy:
Start with your own bank. Ask what the check-writing and transfer restrictions are, what the current interest rate is, and what the average rate was for last year. Compare with several other banks. Make certain the bank you use is federally insured. If rates drop, write a check and move your money elsewhere.

U.S. Treasury Issues

If you would like an investment that requires no research, demands no special expertise, pays competitive rates, and is high in safety, then look to Uncle Sam.

The government provides three virtually risk-free investments in addition to U.S. EE Savings Bonds: Treasury bills, notes, and bonds. All three are backed by the government's full faith and credit. In addition, the interest you earn is exempt from state and local taxes but not from federal income tax. That means, if you're in a high-tax state, your net result could be higher than with a CD or taxable money fund.

Your investment choice will be based on how much you have to invest and for how long you wish to invest. We'll begin with U.S. Treasury notes.

- *U.S. Treasury Notes* mature in one to ten years and pay a fixed rate of interest twice a year. The longer the note's maturity, the higher the interest rate. The minimum investment is $1,000 for notes maturing in four years or more and $5,000 for those maturing in under four years.
- *U.S. Treasury bonds* are a long-term version of T-notes. They mature in ten years or more, with 30 generally being the longest they run. Like T-notes, they are sold with a stated rate of interest, which is paid twice a year. The minimum investment is $1,000.
- *U.S. Treasury bills* are the shortest-term debt obligations sold by the Treasury. Unlike T-notes and bonds, they do not pay interest twice a year. Instead they operate like EE Savings Bonds and sell at a discount from face value. At maturity you receive the full face value. Bills mature in 13, 26, or 52 weeks. The minimum investment is $10,000, with $5,000 increments.

To buy:
T-notes, bonds, and bills are sold by commercial banks, Federal Reserve Banks and branches, stockbrokers, or by mail directly from the Bureau of Public Debt in Washington. Because a broker will charge a fee, ranging anywhere from $25 to $75, you should buy Treasuries directly from the Federal Reserve, one of its branches, or from the Bureau of Public Debt.

To get the current yield on Treasuries and directions on how to buy them direct, call your nearest Federal Reserve Bank, or 202-874-4000.

How To Buy Treasury Securities (free)
Publication # PDP 009

Bureau of Public Debt
1300 C Street SW
Washington, DC 20239

Beginning Investor's Primer

A graduation gift, a tax refund, a savings account that has grown—when you've piled up a sum that's significant in your savings account, move it into one of these safe, higher yielding investments.

Investment	Where to Buy / Invest	Questions to Ask
Money market deposit account	Bank, S&L, Credit Union	What is the interest rate? How often does it change? May I write checks?
Certificate of deposit	Bank, S&L, Credit Union	How much money will I have at maturity? What is the early withdrawal penalty? Are you federally insured?
Money market mutual fund	Brokerage Firm, Mutual Fund	What is the yield? Can I write checks? Must I maintain a minimum?
EE Savings Bonds	Bank, Federal Reserve, Bureau of Public Debt	What is the current rate? How long must I hold the bonds to get that rate?
Treasury issues	Federal Reserve Banks & branches; broker, Bureau of Public Debt	What is the current rate? How do I redeem early? What is the purchase fee?

PART THREE

Your Housing

Frost's definition of home is especially accurate if you're paying the rent or the mortgage. It may also be true if you return to your parents' house. But once you leave the protective environment of your college dorm or childhood bedroom, you'll have to face reality, find shelter, and pay for it. Here's how.

"A place, where, when you go there, they have to take you in."

Robert Frost

8 Boomeranging: Moving Back Home

Thomas Wolfe may have written that "you can't go home again," but thousands of your contemporaries are proving him wrong. Many of the 20- and 30-something crowd are "boomeranging" every year. You may indeed want to be independent, running your own show, taking care of your apartment, car, and clothes, yet a soft job market, extremely high rents, or the need to return to school may take you back home. Or, you may simply need some time to plan your next career move, find yourself and what you want to do. Sometimes re-roosting is a welcome haven when you've lost a job or had a failed romance or a divorce. Sometimes it is simply expected, a matter of your family's lifestyle, in which children live at home until they are married or move out on their own.

Returning home can be a positive experience—it offers you and your parents a chance to develop a close, adult relationship, to enjoy one another as individuals. But it must be handled thoughtfully to avoid straining family relationships and even retarding or hurting your personal growth. Living harmoniously with your parents at this point in your life (and theirs) is contingent on many factors, some of which you can control, some of which you cannot. You can ease the way if you let your family know you plan to pitch in, to act not as their little child, but as an adult. That means cooking, shopping, gardening, doing laundry, walking the dog, cleaning, and paying rent. Unless you are willing to do these things, you cannot expect to be treated as an adult.

Survival Tactics for Living Again with Mom and Dad

It's almost impossible not to feel 12 years old again when you walk back into your old room and eyeball the artifacts of childhood on the shelves, tacked to the walls, hanging in the closet. Even more sticky is trying to redefine your role—to confront issues like money, lifestyle, and privacy.

The best formula for success is to draw up some guidelines *before* you move back home. Make out an informal contract with your parents, covering these points:

- *Room and board.* Offer to fork over some of your take-home pay for room and board. If you don't have a job, substitute additional household work and make a plan to pay when you do have income. Chipping in puts you on an adult footing and avoids fostering any feeling/attitude that you're a charity case. Of course, not all parents will accept money from live-in adult children, but offer anyway. You may be unaware of their financial needs. Don't assume that you may move in with all the perks of childhood and none of the responsibilities of an adult.

- *Household chores.* When you were living with roommates in a dorm or apartment, you shared housekeeping tasks. So, too, it is when you return home. Draw up a list and then don't shirk on your commitments.

- *Guests and friends.* It is your parents' house, and you will have to abide by their rules and values. Bring home friends only after getting approval from your parents. Throw parties only with their prior approval. If they nix either, you'll have to wait until you have your own place. The same goes for smoking and drinking—don't bring them into the house if your parents are against them. In the interest of good health, you shouldn't be using either, anyway.

- *Sex.* If you find it difficult to raise this topic with your parents, then it's probably not a good idea to carry on a romance under their roof. Even the most liberal parents can be surprisingly conservative when it comes to their own kids and sex—they know it happens but they're not quite sure they want to know it.

- *Leaving.* Set a target departure date before moving back in—it could be three months after college graduation or six months after a divorce. Although the date may need to be modified, make it your personal goal to meet it. A deadline will motivate you to get a job or to save money, if you need motivation, and it lets everyone know you're no longer a kid but an adult seeking gainful employment and independence. If moving day arrives and you haven't found a new place to live, make plans to live with a friend, stay at the local "Y", or, if you absolutely must, stay a bit longer, but keep it to one or two months, max. (If the custom in your family is for the children to live at home until they are married, then your wedding day will be your departure date.)

If You're at Home to Help an Aging or Ill Parent
- *Talking with Your Aging Parents* by Mark A. Edinberg; Boston: Shambhala Publications, 1988; $9.95.
- *You and Your Aging Parent* by B. Silverstone & H.K. Hyman; New York: Pantheon, 1990; $14.95.
- *How To Choose A Home Care Agency*; free from:

National Association for Home Care
519 C Street NE
Washington, DC 20002
202-547-7424

• National Council on Aging

409 Third Street SW
Washington, DC 20024
800-424-9046

Preventing Dependency

When adult children move back in with parents, there's a tendency for everyone to revert to earlier family roles, with the result that you become the child again. You want to keep your move back to the old homestead from inadvertently slipping into a long-range situation in which you become emotionally or financially dependent upon your parents. The best way to prevent this is to develop personal and career-oriented goals as well as a financial plan for yourself. Look at your budget after you've been living home a month or two—are you saving money or just enjoying a free ride? Are you spending more on clothes and entertainment than when you were living on your own or at school? If you are, then boomeranging is simply giving you the luxury to spend cash as it comes in. This is a golden opportunity to save a lot of money, whether you're paying rent or not. So, be clear in your own mind that you are back home temporarily while you look for work, finish school, save money, or get your life into first gear, and not to avoid growing up and taking care of yourself.

Even the government has a position on boomeranging—the IRS will categorize you as a dependent if your parents provide more than half of your support. And, as tempting as it is to take money from your parents, in most cases if you do, you will be giving up some degree of control over that aspect of your life, and perhaps others as well. So set limits on the amount of financial support involved between you. Of course, there are times when you may really need to borrow—if, for instance, you've lost your job, if you are between school and work, or if you are raising a child on your own. If your parents can afford to help you out during such periods in your life, they will probably be glad to, but remember that if you do borrow from them, they may feel they have the right to be more involved in your life, especially when it comes to how you spend their loan. You should always regard a parental loan the same way you regard a bank loan—it has to be paid back.

The Privacy Issue

Loss of privacy may be the biggest sacrifice you face when moving home—every aspect of your life is known to your parents—whether you come home at 2 A.M., receive a bill from a collection agency, or get a letter from an ex-spouse or ex-lover. Discuss the fact that you will need more privacy than when you were a kid. And, remember, it's your right to refuse to discuss certain issues with them—just politely let them know the boundaries. On the other hand, be smart and behave in a way that doesn't invite prying.

Insurance Matters

In most states the law considers children to be adults at age 18, 19, or 21—at that point one can vote, run for office, and sign contracts. But if you live at home, it's possible your parents can be held responsible for any property damage or personal injuries that you or your friends cause. Make certain you and your parents discuss these points with the family insurance agent.

Personal Liability
In most states, parents are liable for injuries at a party held in their house even if the party involves you and your friends. Liability can range from medical bills to huge sums in the case of the loss of a life or serious medical damage. Check with your family lawyer regarding your state's specific rulings.

Health Insurance
Generally a parent's health plan at work covers children until they reach age 19, or at least 23 if they are full-time students. After that, federal law requires companies with 20 or more employees to continue health coverage for children over the policy's age limit for up to 36 months, but it's usually very expensive.

After the 36 months, if you don't have your own job and coverage, you'll need to buy your own short-term health policy.

Automobile Insurance
If you own your own car, you will have already obtained insurance. However, if you are driving the family car, offer to help pay for the increased cost of covering a younger driver. And, always fill the tank after using it, pay your own tolls, and offer to foot the bill for some of the repairs. You may even want to buy your parents' car if it's old or they're getting a new one.

Although home, as Robert Frost said, is "a place where, when you go there, they have to take you in," it's definitely not a good idea to arrive on your parents' doorstep with your dirty laundry, old jalopy, and CD player without letting them know of your intention to move back in. You're much more likely to be greeted with hugs if you talk over your housing needs in advance of your arrival. And, don't automatically assume that your parents, no matter how much they love you, will want to give up their independence and space any more than you do.

9 Renting an Apartment, Room, or House

You want to arrange things so your comings-in (your salary) is plentiful enough to meet thy landlord's rent and have lots left over to pay for eating, dressing, playing, traveling, and saving.

Sooner or later you'll be living on your own—if you aren't already—and the first time you do, you'll probably rent an apartment or a room, although ideas about what constitutes housing vary widely. Some members of the 20-something crowd hold rather nontraditional viewpoints about where to live. Mellissa Sanders of Indianapolis, for instance, found life in a little room measuring 6 feet by 7 feet at the top of a pole so comfortable that she stayed for 516 days. The best part—her rent was zilch. Although pole sitting is not a viable solution for most of us, you may indeed think twice about it when you learn how much landlords dare charge for what's advertised as a luxury studio with amenities that turns out to be barely the size of the bedroom you slept in as a child.

> "What are thy rents? What are thy comings-in?"
>
> *Shakespeare*

Yet, despite its cost, the apartment you finally rent is yours and with it comes something wonderful: privacy.

How Much to Pay

Someone once described an apartment as a place to go to change clothes in order to go somewhere else. If this is true for you, you won't need to spend a fortune on rent. On the other hand, if you crave space, love to entertain, or if you work at home, you'll need more than just a changing room. But be careful . . . before beginning your apartment hunt, figure out what you can afford, write it down, and stick to the amount. Never pay more than 30% (ideally, 25%) of your net (take-home) income for rent. If you do, you'll be rent-poor and unable to take that ski vacation, update your wardrobe, or buy a car.

Finding the Right Place

The best way to locate an apartment is through word of mouth; the second, through ads in the newspaper. Tell family, friends, and colleagues that you are looking and where you'd like to land. Post notices on bulletin boards at school, work, your club, place of worship, and at the same time read any notices you see advertising places for rent. If you know the neighborhood in which you want to live and are willing to do a little leg work, walk the area on a regular basis, looking for buildings with "for rent" signs and asking doormen and superintendents about forthcoming vacancies. Ask if you can put your name on a waiting list.

If, on the other hand, you're moving to an area about which you know very little, stay with a friend or relative (offer to pay room and board) or at the "Y" for a few weeks while launching your search. This buys you more time, lets you find your way around the new locale, and relieves the pressure of making a housing decision too quickly.

If you don't find an apartment by word of mouth or through newspaper ads, or if you're simply too busy to do your own legwork, turn to an agent specializing in rentals, sometimes called an apartment finder. These are generally independents not employed by any one landlord. A good agent/finder will save you time and often has access to apartments that are not advertised. Most work for a number of landlords and show apartments for which they will receive compensation from the landlord or management companies, although there are all kinds of arrangements in this field.

Deciphering Rental Babble

a/c = air conditioning	htd = heated
apls = appliances	lndry = laundry
blc = balcony	lrg = large
bs = brownstone	mod = modern
ch = coach house	oc-vu = ocean view
cnvrt = convertible	pkg = parking
clst = closet	riv/v = river view
crptg = carpeting	sec = security deposit
dd = damage deposit	sm = small/tiny
dlx = deluxe	spcs = spacious
ef = efficiency	studio = one room apt
eik = eat-in kitchen	vic = vicinity
f/a = forced air	vu = view
f/lmr = first & last months' rent	wbf = word burning fireplace
fpl = fireplace	wf = wood floors

In your search you may also encounter property management companies that provide full services for the owner, receiving a monthly fee from the landlord.

They keep the building clean, order maintenance

and repairs, collect rents, keep the books, advertise and show apartments, check applicants, and sign leases. A management company often represents a number of owners and so has a larger selection of places than the single owner.

 Be wary of anyone who offers you a lease on the spot. Legitimate landlords always want time to run a credit check and contact your references.

Running the Water

When you find an apartment you like and can afford, look at it at least twice: once in full daylight and once at night. Walk around the neighborhood both times, checking for grocery stores and pharmacies, nearby parking, access to the bus, subway, or highway, cash machines. Do you feel safe? Happy? Once inside the building, ask to see the public spaces—the lobby, laundry room (if any), stairwells, elevator(s), garbage areas, and storage rooms. Are they clean? Is there a doorman? If not, how are guests and delivery people admitted? If there's a pool, game room, or other amenity, is it crowded? Is it secure (restricted to tenants and their guests)? Is there a fee to use it? Other points to check: how recently the elevator has been inspected, the presence of smoke detectors and fire extinguishers, exposed wiring, signs of leaks.

Take time to talk to other residents of the building about the management, superintendent, neighborhood. Have there been any break-ins? A bug or rodent infestation? Are such problems quickly resolved?

An Inside Checklist

1. Note how many locks there are on the door. Are they top-quality?

2. See if there are iron bars or security devices if the apartment is off a terrace, fire escape, or on a low level.

3. Turn on all of the lights.

4. Run hot and cold water in all sinks and tubs; run the shower and flush the toilet at the same time.

5. Open the refrigerator and freezer.

6. Check the dishwasher.

7. Turn on all stove burners, the oven, and the microwave.

8. Turn on the window air conditioners.

9. Try the heat/air conditioning thermostat.

10. Open all cabinets, doors, drawers, closets.

11. Open the windows. Are there screens and storm windows or double panes? When the windows are open, how much noise do you hear from the street?

12. Listen for noise from the next apartment or upstairs. (One reason to visit an apartment at night is to check the noise level when people are home from work.)

The Lease Application

After you find the right apartment, the landlord will ask you to fill out a fairly detailed application. He wants to make certain you can pay the rent and that you're reliable, in order to protect his property as well as the other tenants. Among the items you may be asked for: business and personal references (if you're a first-time renter, give your employer, a nearby relative, your family's lawyer, and/or accountant as references); the name, address, and telephone number of your employer; your current and previous addresses and how long you lived there; the name and location of your bank; your credit cards; your income; divorce payments and loans; your Social Security number; your marital status; and the names of others living in the apartment. (Some states or localities limit the number of unrelated people that can live in an apartment; check with your local housing authority.)

Although you can be turned down for insufficient income (most landlords insist that your monthly gross income be equal to at least three times the rent) or a poor credit record, federal law protects you from being discriminated against on the basis of race, religion, national origin, sex, or disability. Your state's laws may protect you against being banned on the basis of marital status, military status, parental status, source of income, age, political affiliation, or sexual orientation.

Discrimination Laws
If you believe that you have encountered discrimination, contact your state attorney general's office, local housing commission, or call The U.S. Department of Housing and Urban Development's (HUD) hot line, 800-669-9777.

You may be asked to pay for a credit check as well as leave an application deposit, typically one month's rent. If so, get receipts and ask to have in writing the conditions under which this money will be returned. In most localities if you are rejected by the landlord for insufficient income, your application fee or deposit must be returned.

The Lease and Deposit

After the landlord runs a credit check and contacts your references, you will receive the lease. If you haven't established a credit history, if your job situation is shaky, or you have insufficient income, the landlord may insist that you get someone to cosign the lease—that is, to guarantee the rent. The most logical cosigner would be one or both of your parents.

Be prepared to write a check for the first and last months' rent and possibly another month's rent as a security deposit. Find out if you need a certified check and, if so, be sure to get one at your bank ahead of time. The law often requires the landlord to place your security deposit in a separate, interest-bearing account. So ASK.

The lease is a binding contract between you and the landlord, spelling out the responsibilities of both. It cannot be changed while it is in effect unless both parties agree. A lease may be oral or written. However, in many states an oral lease for more than one year cannot be enforced. Make certain all the items agreed upon between you and the landlord are included, such as if you can have your cat, if you can put in your own refrigerator or air conditioner. If the landlord has agreed to repair any problems you uncovered in your inspection, have this spelled out in the lease. If he will not do repairs and you still take the apartment, draw up a list of things in need of repair, date the memo, and include it with your lease, keeping a copy for yourself. If the apartment is furnished, list all the furnishings with a description of their condition and attach it to the lease. Then, when you move out you cannot be charged for any damages.

Most leases run one or two years. A longer lease, of course, protects you from rent increases but at the same time locks you in. If you think you may be transferred or will go back to school in another city within a year, then opt for a one-year lease or make certain you can sublease.

Read carefully the terms concerning subleasing. If you need to move before the lease is up, you want to be able to sublet and then have your parents' lawyer or a lawyer you know review the lease before signing. Do not sign a lease that asks you to 1) pay the landlord's legal fees if you wind up in court; 2) that waives your right to a jury trial; 3) that allows the landlord to take possession of the apartment without giving you notice to vacate; and 4) that requires you to pledge your household furniture as security.

With any item that is to be deleted in the lease, a line is drawn through the clause, and the deletion must be initialed by the landlord and by you in the margin. Make certain this is done on all copies of the lease.

Bear in mind that the rent can be raised when a lease is renewed or when a new one is written. In some areas, the law determines how much the rent can be increased when the lease is renewed and/or if the landlord made repairs between tenants.

 If an apartment has not been rented for some time and/or the market is slow, you may be able to negotiate and get a lower rent, new appliances, or some renovation.

Renewing and/or Leaving

Some leases contain an automatic renewal clause unless you, the tenant, give a 30- or 60-day termination notice. Because this can be a trap for unwary tenants, some states require landlords to give tenants advance notice of the existence of an automatic renewal clause.

On the other hand, you may be required to request a renewal—the terms will be spelled out in your lease. In some cases you may stay in the apartment beyond the terms of the lease on what is known as a "month to month" basis. If so, you must give the landlord (and he, you) at least one month's notice before moving out.

But what if you are transferred to a new city or are accepted at graduate school and need to move?

Breaking a lease is usually quite difficult, if not impossible. However, if the apartment is attractive and likely to rent easily, and your landlord is decent, he may let you out of the contract. You can help by finding an acceptable new tenant. If you cannot, then try negotiating with the landlord, offering to pay his cost of finding a new tenant or forfeiting your security deposit.

Return of your security deposit is determined by state and local laws. In general, if you pay your rent on time and leave the apartment as you found it, you are entitled to a full refund. If you do not pay on time, leave before the lease expires, make unauthorized changes to the property, or do anything else that requires major repairs or cleanup, the landlord can keep your entire deposit, or part of it. In some cities and states you are entitled to a refund with interest.

Always protect yourself when leaving an apartment by taking a video or photos of it, showing that the floors and stove are clean, the refrigerator is empty, that picture and mirror holes have been filled in, and that all light fixtures are in place. Make sure that the photos or videos carry dates.

Subleasing

Sometimes you can find a great living arrangement by subleasing. Perhaps a friend is moving to a new location and wants out of his lease. In that case you take over the remainder of the lease, provided you meet the financial requirements of the landlord.

When looking at a co-op sublet, ask up front how long you will be allowed to sublease and whether you need board approval. If you do, that means being interviewed by several members of the board and giving them letters of reference about your character as well as your finances.

In most states, it's much easier to sublet a condominium—there's no board approval and long-term sublets are not unusual.

Renting Rooms

Don't overlook renting one or two rooms in someone's house—this is often an excellent short-term housing solution, and the cost is considerably lower than that for a separate apartment. And you may wind up with a landlord who bakes cookies. But check it out carefully—will you be able to come and go as you please? Will you have kitchen privileges or be forced to eat out all the time? Can you park your car in the driveway? Will you have adequate privacy? If your landlord is elderly, housebound, or disabled, you may be able to reduce the rent in exchange for shopping or doing other errands for him or her—but have the details spelled out in writing first—you don't want to wind up doing more than you bargained for.

Roommates

You thought you were finished with roommates the day you graduated or stopped sharing a bedroom with your brother or sister, but they may be part of your life once again when it comes time to pay the rent. If you can't afford to live by yourself, if you want more space, or if you simply prefer to have company around, roommates are ideal.

The Ideal Roommate Is:
- Employed or has income
- Honest
- Compatible
- Communicative
- Flexible
- Tactful
- Willing to share

The best roommate is someone you already know, who is responsible and trustworthy. If you don't know someone with whom to room, check the roommate ads in newspapers, the notices on work and school bulletin boards, or by using a matching service. Take time to interview potential roommates very carefully. It is crucial to find someone you not only like but whom you trust—after all, you'll be sharing living space as well as financial responsibilities. Trust your instincts, and if there's anything offputting about the person, do not room with him or her.

Plan to meet for coffee near the apartment, or where you work. If you hit it off, then look at the apartment together. (If you already have an apartment and are looking for a roommate, do not invite a stranger in without first meeting him/her elsewhere.)

You (and/or) the landlord will want to check the potential roommate's business references, income, and credit rating. (Personal references are almost always likely to be biased and not sufficient for judging a stranger's character.)

All roommates' names should be on the lease and on any other documents you sign, so you will be collectively responsible for paying the rent and taking good care of the property. Each roommate writes his or her individual deposit check and then individual monthly checks to the landlord.

Once you have settled on a roommate, discuss the key financial and personal issues involved in sharing space, such as privacy—for example, is it alright to have a boyfriend or girlfriend sleep over, and for how long, and at what point should this person contribute to the cost of shared food? How will you pay for utilities, food, and household items—the easiest way is to divide costs evenly, but if one of you dines out more than the others, then make adjustments. Arrange to keep a log of generally shared expenses (such as for household cleaning items and basic food staples), total it once a month, and divide the cost evenly. Determine, too, how to pay for furnishings.

Roommates generally arrive with some of their own stuff, but you may need to purchase a sofa, rug, or coffee table. In the long run it's easiest if one roommate makes the purchase so he can take it with him when he eventually leaves the situation. However, you may need to pool money to buy a major item; if so, keep the receipt and a record of your joint purchase.

Then, when one of you leaves, the other can buy his share; or, you may decide to sell it to a third party and divide the proceeds.

You'll also need to determine whether to have separate telephone lines or share, tracking long distance calls and splitting the basic monthly charge.

Handling Long Distance Yakity Yak
Instead of dividing the long distance telephone bill among roommates, sign up with your phone-service provider to have calls tallied separately. Each roommate gets a two-digit code to punch in when dialing, and charges are arranged on the bill by code. There's no fee. AT&T: 800-222-0400.

Other roommate considerations: If you come in late, do so quietly. Don't pry or meddle into your roommate's life. Don't hog the bathroom, and make sure it's clean when you leave. Do your share of the cleaning and shopping. Take messages. Be polite to your roommate's parents and other visitors.

Don't always accept invitations from the roommate's parents for dinner—they would probably like some time with their son or daughter alone now and then, as much as they may like you, too. Don't borrow your roommate's clothes, CD player, or anything else without asking first. And, respect his/her right not to lend items.

Renter's Insurance

You may have furnished your apartment in Early Salvation Army, yet replacing these pieces, your clothes, TV, jewelry, and microwave would be very expensive. Your landlord's insurance does not cover your furniture nor any other contents of the apartment, so you should purchase renter's insurance. Because you are just starting out on your own, you may view your situation as somewhat temporary, yet it's a mistake not to get coverage—leaks, fires, and thefts are unfortunately not all that uncommon, and they can be devastating.

Take out a policy that will cover at least 80% of the replacement cost of your possessions. If you have a computer, fax, or other office equipment in a home-based office, talk to your agent about insuring them separately, if necessary, through a home office rider.

> **Replacement Cost**
> The value of a lost or damaged item based on what it costs to replace the item today.

If you're a big party giver, you may want to have a rider added to your policy for "host liquor" coverage, protecting you against lawsuits from enthusiastic guests who, after leaving your wingding, are involved in an alcohol-related accident.

> **Rider**
> An additional provision that modifies or amends the basic insurance policy; it may increase or decrease benefits or make other changes; also known as an endorsement or attachment.

Covering Valuables

> **Floater**
> An amendment to your insurance policy that provides coverage for specific property, such as a personal computer, jewelry, or boat; it is called a floater because it follows the movement of the specific property insured.

If you have your grandmother's silver tea service, your father's antique watch, a stamp collection, or other valuables, get a separate floater providing extra coverage for certain stated valuables. Unless you've just purchased them and have the sales receipt, have a professional appraise them. Make certain you have "all-risk" coverage in your floater policy, so you will be reimbursed no matter how your valuables were lost.

All Risk
A policy that covers every risk it doesn't specifically exclude.

Some floater policies have a "named-peril" basis, in other words, the insurance company will reimburse you only when the type of loss is listed (or "named") in the policy. . .so if your loss is caused by a natural disaster or something else not listed in the policy, you'll get zip reimbursement.

Personal Inventory

If you purchase insurance (and even if you don't), it's a good idea to have a personal inventory of your possessions. Take photos or a video of all furniture, paintings, posters, appliances you own, TVs, computers, rugs, good clothing and jewelry, and anything else of value. Record serial numbers for all appropriate items, along with a description.

What To Put In Your Fireproof Evacuation File Box:
- Inventory of your belongings
- Videotape/photos of possessions
- Your lease
- Insurance policies
- Auto papers: registration, copy of driver's license, purchase papers, note of plate numbers, insurance coverage form
- Copies of birth certificate, passport, school records, copy of will, list of credit card numbers
- List of investments: CDs and bank accounts
- Copies of state and federal tax returns for the last five years

Make a copy of your inventory and photos and store one somewhere other than in your house—in your bank safe-deposit box, at your office, or parents' house—and the second copy in your fireproof "evacuation file." Update both as you acquire possessions, sell them, or give them away.

Read:
"Disaster Preparation." Free from: California Society of Enrolled Agents, 3200 Ramos Circle, Sacramento, CA 95827; 916-366-6646.

PART FOUR

Your Shopping

Yet if you've got enough of them you can shop until you drop—not something we particularly recommend—but you will need to buy food, furniture, clothes, perhaps a car or motorcycle, and eventually a house.

"A nickel goes a long way now. You can carry it around for days without finding a thing it will buy."

Anon.

10 *Wheels*

Best Ways to Drive Home a Bargain

The glorious sense of freedom and independence that comes with acquiring your first car is one of life's marvelous and rarely duplicated experiences. That same experience also introduces one to the art of negotiating, getting a loan, handling debt, buying insurance, and dealing with the red tape of registration.

Whether you're going for your first set of wheels or replacing an older car, pickup, or van, you want to know you got the best price possible when you head out of the lot and down Route 66. You also want to have purchased a safe car, one you can easily afford and that won't drive you into the poor house.

"A car is an invention which makes people go fast and money go faster."

Jimmy Lyons

> **For Great Car Tips**
> Read: *Nutz & Boltz*, Box 123, Butler, MD 21023; monthly; $25/year; 410-584-7574.

The automobile industry is known for fast-talking salespeople, but the recession and a slower sales pace have changed even that—somewhat. All of GM's Saturn dealers and some thousand other new-car dealers, for example, have begun so-called one-price selling. The best way to take advantage of these and other buying trends is by being an informed, rational buyer, not one swept away by emotion who falls in love with the hottest, most expensive car on the lot.

How Much Car You Can Afford

Before you visit that first showroom, establish the total monthly cost of owning a car—include monthly finance charges, registration, taxes, insurance, and maintenance. You'll have to set aside a couple of weeks and some telephone time to gather the facts. Then, note the total figure on a piece of paper and put it into your wallet. Remember it's there when you go car shopping and stick to the written dollar amount. At this point—before you decide to buy—perhaps you should consider leasing.

Pricey Facts

The average new car costs between $16,000 and $17,000.

The most expensive standard car is the Rolls Royce 8-cylinder Phantom VI, which sells for about $595,000.

The most expensive car to build: the Presidential 1969 Lincoln—21 feet, 6.3 inches long, with 12,000 tons of armor plate and weighing 12,000 pounds. If all four tires are shot out, it can still travel at 50 mph on inner rubber-edged steel discs.

The most expensive used car: a 1931 Bugatti Type 41 Royal Sports Coupe was sold for $9,845,000 in 1987 to Nicholas Harley, a London car dealer.

Used cars

The minute you drive a new car off the lot you've lost at least $2,000. By the end of the year your purchase will have depreciated by nearly 30%. That should tell you that a good used car is one way to get more for your money—it not only costs less, it's less expensive to insure and it loses its value more slowly. Check the annual *Consumer Reports Buying Guide* and the *Blue Book* for information and prices on the best used car models. *Consumer Reports* also has a valuable, updated list of used cars to avoid.

Buying a used car is a tricky business—prices vary, paint covers a myriad of flaws, and odometers are changed to misrepresent the number of miles a car has been driven. But the potential savings over a new car make it well worthwhile investigating. Often it's more fun and easier to do with a knowledgeable friend in tow.

Consumer Reports Used-Car Price Service quotes purchase and trade-in prices over the telephone for 1984 to date cars and light trucks. Calls cost $1.75/minute and take about 5 minutes. Before calling, know the model name or number, year, mileage, number of cylinders, options, and overall condition. 900-446-1120.

Tips for buying a used car

- Four-door sedans and station wagons get less wear and tear than other models.
- Convertibles, sports, and luxury models command the highest prices and the highest repair bills.
- It's best to buy from someone you know.
- Ask a private dealer why they are selling.
- Late models with low mileage are usually found at a dealer, where they have been traded in; although

the price will be higher than with a private seller, you can usually get a warranty.

- Check a dealership with your Better Business Bureau.
- Have your mechanic examine it.
- Demand the vehicle's title. The owner may still owe money on it; if so, call the lender before giving the seller any money above a modest deposit.
- Ask to see the car's service records.

Rental Cars For Sale
- Hertz, 800-654-3131
- Avis, 800-331-1212
- National, 800-328-4567

Warning signs of trouble in used cars

- Blue smoke
- Rusty coolant
- Fresh welding
- Rust on the body
- Mismatched colors
- Puddles or stains underneath car
- New undercoating
- Greenish white stains on radiator cap
- Uneven, worn tire treads
- Metal shavings in transmission fluid
- Musty odor inside car
- Lumpy, sagging driver's seat

Rental cars

Used cars can also be purchased from Avis, Hertz, National, and other car rental companies. Their 10- to 18-month old cars have nonnegotiable, yet below retail, prices. Ask for a maintenance record for the car before buying and show it to your mechanic. One particular advantage: they've had regular servicing. Try to get a limited warranty. Call the toll-free numbers for the nearest location.

Demonstration cars

Lent to salespeople for showing to prospective buyers and/or for their personal use, these cars are often sold after six months or so at 15 to 20% off. Get one that's still covered by the manufacturer's warranty and ask if it can be extended for a small fee.

Test driving a car

Before buying any car, new or used, give it a good half- to three-quarters hour workout, taking it on bumpy roads, in stop-and-go-traffic and on highways. Be sure to turn on the lights and wipers, air conditioner and heater. Listen for pings, knocks, catches, and bucking. Test the brakes at 45 mph.

Lemon Laws
Since the early 1980s every state except South Dakota has passed a lemon law, but some are so weak they barely count. If you think you bought a lemon (a faulty vehicle), read Ralph Nader's *The Lemon Book* (Moyer Bell, 1990) to learn how to file complaints and prepare your case for court.

Once you've found a car you think you like, come back another day and take a second test drive. This time hire a good mechanic and bring him/her along. If it's a used car, call the National Highway Traffic Safety Administration (800-424-9393) to see if the model has been recalled. If so, get proof that it's been fixed or forget it.

Finding a Good Mechanic
The American Automobile Association has a nation-wide Approved Auto Repair Program that evaluates reliable repair shops. AAA inspectors apply rigorous standards, and more garages fail than pass. Telephone your local club for names in your area or look for the sticker in the shop's window.

Finding The Top Deals On Wheels

The celebrated Model T Ford, introduced on October 1, 1908, originally cost $850 but by 1926 the price, because of efficient manufacturing, had dropped to $310. Unfortunately, car prices have rarely dropped as much ever again, although occasionally prices are cut on slow sellers. You can get a good price if you take your time, get the facts, and put emotions aside.

Four Car Shopping Services
- Amway, 800-992-6929; membership, $34.95; 900+ participating dealers; $50 over factory invoice.
- CarBargains, 800-475-7283; $135 for bids from five dealers in your area.
- Car/Puter, 800-221-4001; there's a $500 nonrefundable deposit, applied to cost of car; some 500 participating dealers; printouts available.
- American Automobile Association—a number of AAA affiliates have set up car-buying services for members; check your area office.

Using a car-buying service

If you have no stomach for shopping and haggling with dealers, turn to one of the national car-buying services who make arrangements with dealers to sell to their members at a discount. Some also sell price sheets or printouts. For somewhere between $75 and $150, depending upon where you live, these firms will canvas dealers in your area on your behalf. After calling a toll-free number you'll get forms in the mail, asking you to specify the car and features you want. You'll wind up paying from $50 to several hundred dollars above the dealer cost for domestic cars—more on imports. Cars purchased this way often come directly from the factory, not the dealer's lot, so plan on up to six to eight weeks for delivery. Or, if the dealer making the sale is not nearby, you may have to pay extra to have the car shipped to a local dealership; ASK.

 Dealer prep and handling should not be part of what you pay, because the factory pays the dealership to prepare a vehicle for delivery.

> **Prep**
> Euphemism for gas, oil, air in the tires.

The no-haggle, no-dicker sticker method

Another way around showroom phobia is to buy from a single-price dealership. Prices are often adjusted periodically, but there's no negotiating. You may not get the rock bottom price, but there's none of the tension involved in trying to talk the salesman down, and this approach saves time. In addition to GM's Saturn division, over a thousand other dealers, representing most makes except top-line luxury cars, set one firm low price that tends to be about $600 to $1,000 below the manufacturer's suggested retail price, but still some $200 to $600 above the dealer's cost.

The old-fashioned art of negotiating

To get the lowest possible price, there's simply no better way than to bargain hard. Here are 10 tips on getting the best price the traditional way:

- Pick your car before negotiating. Visit an auto show or several dealers to determine the car you want. Then test drive it, but don't negotiate until you've got your financing in place (see below).
- Get a bid from a single-price dealership and then go to two or three regular dealers and ask them to beat the offer. Let all of them know you're talking to other dealers.

 Use the price printouts from one of the car shopping services as a base price.

- Don't buy when the volume of unsold cars falls below a 60-day supply (published weekly in *Automotive News*); it's a seller's market and dealers are usually unwilling to dicker.
- Buy a model that is in oversupply. Dealers often offer cash rebates on them.
- Shop at the end of the month; dealers don't like carrying over inventory, and salespeople want to meet their monthly sales quotas and so they are willing to negotiate.
- Shop at the end of the model year or season. Both manufacturers and dealers need to clear the lots to make room for the new models, and they are good bargains at this time.
- Ignore the sticker price. It's the manufacturer's cost plus a dealer profit of 7 to 20%, or even

more. Negotiate based on the dealer's true cost (the factory or dealer invoice) found in *Edmund's New Car Prices* or *Edmund's Import Car Prices* ($4.95 each on newsstands). Your target price should be $100 to $200 over dealer cost on a car costing $10,000 to $15,000; $200 to $400 on a car $15,000 to $18,000; and $400 to $600 for a car in the $18,000 to $25,000 range.

For a printout of invoice and sticker prices and cost of all factory-installed options for any model car, send $11 ($20 for two) to:

Consumer Reports Auto Price Service
  Box 8005
  Novi, MI 48376
  810-347-5810; 800-933-5555

- Check the manufacturer's label on the door on the driver's side to see when the car was made. If it's been on the lot for a while, you're more apt to get the price down.

- Sell your old car before negotiating. It increases your chances for getting the best price for it and prevents the new car dealer from messing up your price negotiations. Check your old car's value in *Edmund's Used Car Prices* or *Kelley Blue Book*, updated several times a year. Place an ad in your local classified pages or sell your car back to the used car department of a dealer who sells the same make. (If your old car is a real wreck, you may do better with a dealer.)

Savings Tip
Separate buying a new car, financing it, and selling your old car. By making these three separate transactions you'll get better prices all around.

Negotiate the price on the new car first and get it in writing; then bring up the fact you have a car to trade in.

- Skip the bells and whistles. Don't run up the cost of your car with items you don't need, such as rustproofing, unnecessarily long warranties, sun roofs, etc.

Cost of Owning a New Car

According to the American Automobile Association, the annual cost of operating the most popular cars is just a little over $3,000. That assumes you drive 15,000 miles per year with no more than 10 miles to or from work. Gasoline is figured in at $1.22/gallon, and insurance coverage assumes a $250 deductible for comprehensive, a $500 deductible for collision, and $100,000, $300,000, and $500,000 limits for liability coverage. Interest payments are based on a 10% loan for four years.

Gas and oil	$ 897
Maintenance	348
Tires	132
Insurance	730
License, registration, taxes	229
Interest payments	677
TOTAL ANNUAL COST	$3,013

Smart Financing

The best prices are obtained by the relatively small number of Americans who pay cash for their cars. Most of us, however, finance buying our wheels—and if you fall into that category, read on. Car loans are available at banks, credit unions, and auto dealerships.

Put into operation as many of the following tips as you can to hold down your cost, keeping in mind that the longer the loan, the less the monthly payments, but the more you wind up paying in interest (see table).

Arrange financing before you start shopping. Banks and credit unions will often commit to a loan ahead of time. This is part of knowing what you can afford and sticking to it.

Check out your credit union. Their loans are often about a half-point to a point lower than those offered by banks. Some even help you with negotiations. And, about 1,000 credit unions subscribe to *PC Carbook*, a computerized car-pricing service. Others arrange discounted deals through auto brokers.

Consider a home equity loan. The interest is generally tax deductible and rates tend to be lower than on other types of loans. (Interest on most loans is not deductible.)

Reduce the amount of financing by increasing your down payment.

Avoid F & I. This "financing and insurance" is arranged by the car dealer, but because it is often the most profitable part of the dealership, the salesperson will try to run up the total price with insurance policies attached onto the loan. The cost is often added to the price of the car, so you wind up paying interest on your own insurance premiums.

Look for discounts, rebates, and incentives. One discount you might overlook is buying the floor model. Discounts come from manufacturers and dealers in all shapes and sizes. Rebates are only given by the manufacturer to the buyer—you buy the car, send in the sales slip, and then you get your rebate.

Cost Of A $10,000 Loan At 12% Interest (rounded to nearest dollar)

	5 Years	6 Years
Your monthly payment	$ 222	$ 196
Total interest charges	$ 3,347	$ 4,076
TOTAL COST OF LOAN	$13,347	$14,076

Auto Insurance

You'll need to insure your car, and it will be expensive. Before taking out a policy be familiar with what exactly it is you are buying coverage for.

"Nine Ways to Lower Your Auto Insurance Costs," free from:

Insurance Information Institute
  110 William Street
  New York, NY 10038
  212-669-9250

The basic types of coverage

1. *Bodily injury liability*. Provides money to pay claims against you and the cost of your legal defense if your car injures or kills someone.

2. *Property damage liability*. Provides money to pay claims and defense costs if your car damages the property of others.

3. *Medical payments*. Pays medical expenses resulting from accidental injuries—you and your loved ones as well as other passengers in your car.

4. *Uninsured motorists*. Pays for injuries caused by an uninsured or a hit-and-run driver.

5. *Collision insurance.* Pays for damage to your car resulting from a collision or from overturning.
6. *Comprehensive physical damage.* Pays for damages when your car is stolen or damaged by fire, flooding, hail, or other perils.

States that have "no-fault" insurance laws require personal insurance protection coverage and may also have some restrictions on liability lawsuits. Check with your insurance agent.

Collision and comprehensive coverage are available with a deductible. This means that you agree to pay a specified amount—the first $50, $200, or $500—of damage to your car in each loss and the insurance company will pay the remainder. By eliminating the cost of processing small claims, the company can provide such coverage at a lower price.

Eleven ways to reduce your insurance bill
1. Shop around. Get prices from independent agents who represent many companies, from State Farm which has its own in-house agents, and from at least one direct writer that sells by mail, such as GEICO (800-841-3000) or Worldwide (800-325-1487).
2. Get group rates. If you are or were in the armed forces, call USAA, 800-531-8080.
3. Buy a used car that costs less to insure. You can get a list of vehicles that are charged below-average rates from your insurance companies.
4. Talk to an auto mechanic. They sometimes know which insurance companies are best to deal with.
5. Take the highest deductible possible. Insurance is too expensive to file claims for small losses. On collision and comprehensive you want just

enough to cover losses you can't afford. Raising deductibles to $200, $500, or $1,000 will cut as much as 40% from collision and comprehensive bills.

6. Skip some coverage. If you drive an older car, insurers will not pay out more than its value, even if totally ruined in an accident—don't pay more in collision insurance premiums than your car is worth.

7. Get discounts. Available to nonsmokers, nondrinkers, graduates of driver education programs, young people with good grades, cars with air bags, good drivers with accident-free records, cars driven less than 7,500 miles/year. Some insurance companies give discounts to drivers in a car pool or to those who insure more than one car with the company, or insure their car and house with the same company. An ignition cutoff system and/or a hood-locking or wheel-locking device may get a discount. Members of some professions, such as doctors and lawyers who are regarded as good risks, get discounts. And, remind your parents that discounts are available to those 50 or 55 years or older and to members of AARP.

8. Just say "no" to unnecessary options if they duplicate protection you already have such as life insurance, disability pay, coverage for towing, and theft insurance. If you need more insur-

---

Beat the rating game. Young drivers generally pay higher insurance rates—often until age 25 for women and 30 for men. You might get a 30% lower rate by foregoing your own car and have your parent be the principal driver.

ance, beef up your life insurance policy—it's probably cheaper and you don't have to die in a car accident for heirs to collect. In some no-fault states, personal injury protection already provides a death benefit. Your job may provide disability insurance, and your homeowners' policy may cover contents of your car that are stolen.

9. Pick the right car. Models that thieves favor, sports cars and all luxury models, cost more to insure. Your insurance company can provide a list of discounted cars.

10. File small claims only if there's a chance someone has been hurt. It's too expensive to file for damage under a few hundred dollars, and it drives up your rates.

11. Pay your premiums annually if you can; installment plans are convenient but wind up costing you more because of the interest added on.

Loaning Out Your Car

Humorist, author, and mother and grandmother of many drivers, Erma Bombeck offers this advice: "Never lend your car to anyone to whom you have given birth." Nor should you give your car to anyone else unless you know for a fact that he/she:

- has a valid drivers license
- is covered by insurance
- is a safe driver
- does not drink and drive
- does not do drugs and drive

Automobile Clubs

If you hate to change a tire, get your hands dirty, or use jumper cables, look into an automobile club that will rescue you if you're stranded with a disabled car. Three national clubs that will send help are: American Automobile Association (800-222-4357), Amoco Motor Club (800-334-3300), and Allstate Motor Club (800-255-2582).

Before joining, call and ask all three the same set of questions:

- Do you provide a directory of affiliated service stations?
- How many stations are there?
- How many have 24-hour service?
- What towing and repair costs are covered?
- What is the annual fee? Does it cover all family members?
- Do you provide trip planning? If so, send an example.

 If you never venture very far from home, you may get faster service from a local or regional club. Check your telephone book for names.

Take Your Car Key
A car is stolen every 19 seconds in the United States, and more than 20% had the key in the ignition. For more tips, get a free copy of *How to Keep Your Car from Being Stolen* at your local Shell station, or by calling 800-23-SHELL.

---

11 *Housekeeping*

Nicer clothes, appliances, and other things, provided you budget sensibly and avoid spending sprees. In fact, conspicuous consumption, the rage of the 1980s as chronicled in Tom Wolfe's novel, *Bonfire of the Vanities*, is generally out these days. The arrogant "masters of the universe" have been replaced by the environmentalist greens and more frugal types devoted to quality time and politically correct issues. That doesn't mean you and your friends now must live like puritans or turn into misers. You're still allowed to enjoy imported beer, a smooth running sports coupe (or at least a car that starts when you turn on the ignition), and a week skiing in Colorado or reading on a beach. In this chapter we'll show you over 50 ways to reduce spending on housekeeping matters so you can enjoy the extra dollars you save elsewhere. You must do one thing, however, to make the process work: track the amount you save, even small amounts, and stash them in your savings account on a regular basis.

"Money can't buy friends but it can get you a better class of enemy."

Spike Mulligan

15 Easy Ways Anyone Can Save Money

You may think saving is simply impossible. That you can't cut back on everyday expenses. That you can't manage on your salary. That you need an intricate budget. Not true. Although a budget is a great help and we'll show you how to draw up a simple, foolproof one, you can begin saving right now. Begin by looking at these 15 easy ways to save. You'll be able to put at least a third of them into immediate practice.

1. *Quit smoking.* If you smoke two packs a day at $2/pack, you can save $1,460 in one year. Your life insurance premiums will be slashed and you will live longer, which will cost you more, but that's life.

2. *Take your lunch to work.* At least now and then. If you're spending $5 a day on a sandwich, coke, and an ice cream cone, that's $1,250 a year, assuming two weeks out for a vacation. If you've got a large appetite and shell out $8 a day, the total is $2,000. And that's not counting those in-between snacks of chips, pretzels, and cappuchino-to-go. Figure out what you spend per day on lunch and on the days you brown bag it, put that amount into your savings account.

A famous miser, Henrietta (Henry) Howland Green, kept a balance of over $31,400,000 in one bank alone. She dined strictly on cold oatmeal because she was too frugal to spend money to heat it. When she died in 1916, her estate was worth $95 million.

Eat in your company cafeteria; most are subsidized and have low prices.

3. *Share newspapers with co-workers.* If you buy the *Wall Street Journal* and your local newspaper every weekday, you're spending close to $300 a year. Split the cost with a friend and save $150 as well as create less to recycle.

4. *Subscribe to magazines.* If you know you're going to buy a newsstand copy every week or month, subscribe. A subscription to *Rolling Stone* for example is $19.95 a year while individual copies are $2.95. Or, share subscriptions.

5. *Use your library.* Check out books, magazines, tapes, and records instead of buying them. (Of course, we're glad you bought this book.)

6. *Buy stamps at the post office.* There's a $3 fee for ordering by phone, using your credit card. Getting stamps from a vending machine at a convenience store is ridiculously expensive—you wind up paying 50 cents for a 29-cent stamp. Use postcards when you can—at 19 cents apiece they're even cheaper than a telephone call.

7. *Buy your phone.* AT&T rates on leased phones are now up to $5/month. That means a basic touch-tone model costs $60/year. Buy a second-hand phone or a new one from a business products catalog or a discount store that comes with a warranty. Having a touch-tone phone is recommended, too, as many places you call often have menus that require you to enter digits.

8. *Talk cheap.* If most of your calls are to a single area code, check out special reduced rate plans offered by the long distance carriers.

9. *Talk cheaper.* Dial direct instead of asking an operator for assistance. And, look up numbers yourself; you'll avoid a charge ranging from 45 to 60 cents for directory assistance. If you use information once a day every day of the year, at 50 cents per inquiry, you're spending close to $200 a year.

10. *Pump your own gas.* You'll save about 18 cents per gallon.

11. *Drive at the speed limit.* Driving at 70 mph instead of 55 means a fuel loss of as much as 35%, so gas you paid $1.20/gallon for actually cost you $1.62.

12. *Clip coupons.* If you save $15 a month with food and drug coupons, that's $180 a year; $25 a month turns into $300. (The average coupon is worth 58 cents.)

13. *Buy wash-and-wear clothes.* Dry cleaning is very pricey.

14. *Don't pay a babysitter.* Set up a co-op service with friends and neighbors.
And finally,

15. *Don't carry much cash.* If you leave your ATM card, your credit card, your debit card, your checkbook, and most of your cash at home, it will be hard to spend very much.

When To Say "Hello"
To cut long distance bills, sign up for a discount plan. Go over the last three months of bills, listing frequently called numbers and how much you spent. Send the most typical bill to these two carriers:

- MCI Customer Service
  1200 S. Hayes Street
  Arlington, VA 22202
  800-444-3333
- Sprint Corp.
  Bill Analysis
  10951 Lakeview
  Lenexa, KS 66219
  800-877-4646

and. . .phone your information to:

- AT&T
  800-222-0300

Telephone rates are typically lowest:

- Evenings from 9 to 11 pm and Sundays from 5 to 11 pm when there's a 40% savings.
- Weekday nights, from 11 pm to 8 am, there's a 65% discount.
- Saturday there's a 65% discount all day.
- Sunday from 8 am to 5pm and 11 pm to 8 am there's a 65% discount.
- Holidays—New Year's Day, July 4th, Labor Day, Thanksgiving, and Christmas there's 40% off, and 65% from 11 pm to 8 am.

Controlling Your Spending: A Budget That Makes Sense

Nearly everyone needs to curtail their spending at one time or another. It's easy to splurge in our society where advertising inundates us with information about the latest model cars, the season's fashionable look in clothes, and which vacation spots are trendy. Yet both—curtailing and spending—are just habits, and ones that can be changed. If you need to plug the leaks in your wallet, you'll find it's not so difficult to do once you know where they are.

The key to taking charge of your financial life is to gather the facts and then make a conscious decision to direct exactly where you want your money to go, rather than letting it gently sift away, unaccounted for. To do this you need to take a snapshot of your cash flow and find out where you're funneling money each month. To get started, use the annual cash flow worksheets that follow to track your yearly spending.

It will take a couple of hours to gather the data and plug in the numbers. The majority of information will come from your tax return, checkbook record and/or canceled checks, your bank statements, and your paycheck stubs. To fill in some of the other numbers, you may need to keep a daily expense diary for a month or two to learn where your so-called "walking around money" is going. Buy a small notebook, carry it at all times, and write down what you spend cash on every day. Then simply total it up at the end of the month and multiply by 12. If you think the month was not typical for some reason—you have a new job or have moved, for example, then track spending for another month. You may be quite surprised by the amount siphoned off into impulse purchases such as snacks, taxis, flowers, fast food, magazines, pay telephone calls, etc.

In all categories, forget the pennies and round off to the nearest dollar—otherwise it will take forever, drive you crazy, and you may give up in frustration.

Tracking Your Spending

ANNUAL INCOME

Earnings from job	$_____
Bonuses	$_____
Freelance, consulting, odd jobs	$_____
Interest income; dividend income	$_____
Proceeds from sale of investments	$_____
Gifts, inheritances	$_____
Alimony, child support	$_____
Other	$_____

TOTAL ANNUAL INCOME $_____

(Note: later on in life you would add two items to this list: pension and social security income)

ANNUAL EXPENSES

Housing: rent/mortgage	$_____
Savings	$_____
Utilities (gas, electric, water)	$_____
Telephone	$_____
Real estate taxes	$_____
Food (groceries, snacks)	$_____
Liquor	$_____
Eating out	$_____
Entertainment (movies, tennis, etc.)	$_____
Vacation	$_____
Transportation—bus, taxi, train; bike, car, truck upkeep & gas	$_____
Insurance	$_____
Clothing	$_____
Cosmetics, toiletries	$_____

Exercise class, health club, gym	$_____
Gifts	$_____
Contributions	$_____
Furniture	$_____
Home improvements	$_____
Medical and dental expenses	$_____
Child care and education	$_____
Your education/classes	$_____
Unreimbursed business expenses	$_____
Alimony, child support	$_____
Debt, loan, and credit card payments other than mortgage	$_____
Walking around money	$_____
Club dues/memberships	$_____
Business and professional expenses	$_____
Income taxes	$_____
Social security taxes	$_____
Other	$_____
TOTAL ANNUAL EXPENSES	$_____

After tracing your spending, ideally the bottom line will show a surplus, money that you've managed to save. But if you're like most people starting out, you may be saving very little or just breaking even. That's not bad. In fact it's good. If, on the other hand, your calculations show you're in debt, you need to mend your ways and start spending less, saving more.

Fixed Expenses
Those that remain relatively constant from one month or year to the next, such as mortgage payments, rent, life insurance premiums, child care, utilities, and property taxes.

Ways to rein in spending

For most of us, over half of our income is earmarked for housing, food, taxes, and other fixed, basically immutable expenses. That means you have to cut back in other areas, known as variable expenses. Throughout this chapter you'll find tips for how to do just that. Here are some more savings tips:

- Eat at home.
- Realize that the small stuff adds up—both ways— spending and saving.
- Make only preplanned shopping trips for specific items in order to curtail impulse buying.
- Keep your emotions in rein. Spending habits are often driven in part by psychology. Refrain from buying when you're on a high, when you're worried or angry. Some people even spend out of revenge. Don't be that dumb.
- Avoid shopping malls and department stores when you feel blue; instead, go to a movie, listen to music, jog or take a walk, call a friend.

Once you have set up a working budget (and only YOU can do this—no one can do it for you, just as no one can lose weight for you or improve your job skills) gradually treat yourself to a few luxuries and extras. If you've saved according to plan, paid down a debt, for instance, reward yourself by dining at a favorite restaurant or by going to a concert. As you gain control over your cash flow, you can afford to be kinder, gentler to yourself, to enjoy your budgeting victories and the sense of security that comes from being "master" of your financial universe.

Variable Expenses
Those that are flexible and vary from one month or year to the next. They are more difficult to forecast, but you have more control over them than over fixed expenses. For example, clothing, eating out, vacations, entertainment, and charitable contributions.

How To Be Chic Yet Cheap

Entertaining

You don't have to match the now legendary Malcolm Forbes, who founded the magazine that still bears his name—he spent some $2 million on his 70th birthday party in 1989, flying in Liz Taylor and hundreds of other celebrities for several days of fun and games on the island near Tangier, Morocco. You can have just as much fun in your own back yard or state park.

Here are some ideas for chic, cheap entertaining.

- *Do it yourself.* If you can cook, do. Caterers, plain or fancy, run up the cost of a dinner party. If you can't cook, then bring in take-out food.

Humongous Meat Loaf: How To Serve 50 People For $1 Each

Mix together:

8 ½ pounds ground ham or hamburger
5 ½ pounds lean ground pork
3 ½ cups corn flake crumbs
3 ½ cups milk
4 green peppers, chopped
7 medium onions, minced
4 pints of canned tomatoes
4 eggs

Mix well and pack into three large baking pans. Bake at 350 degrees for two hours.

(Source: Ellen Flaherty)

- *Give a potluck dinner.* This old-fashioned way of entertaining saves time and money. Invite friends, ask each one to bring a part of the meal. As the host or hostess you may want to prepare the entree or the cocktails, wine and coffee. If anyone questions your chic quotient, remind them that the first Thanksgiving was a potluck affair.

- *Go on picnics.* And, again, share the food with others. Or follow what the young crowd does in Chicago: give a BYOB party (bring your own beef). All you need is a grill; let friends cook their own entree and you provide the veggies, drinks, and dessert. (Since too much beef is no longer politically correct or healthy, bring scallops, tuna, and swordfish to grill.

- *Give theme parties.* Invite friends over for wine, cheese, and sandwiches or a gourmet pizza while watching the Superbowl; switch to mint juleps and tea sandwiches for the Kentucky Derby. Another way to forego serving an expensive four-course dinner: have people gather at your place for coffee and dessert after a concert, play, or other event.

Recession Punch: How to Serve 50 People for under $20
Boil for 5 minutes: 2 cups sugar and 1 cup water
Add: 2 cups concentrated fruit punch, 1 cup lemonade, 2 cups orange juice, 2 cups pineapple juice, 2 bottles cheap champagne, 2 quarts ginger ale, 1 quart club soda
(NOTE: Sparkling apple cider may be used instead of champagne for a perfect nonalcoholic alternative.)

Source: Jeffrey L. Pack, St. Louis, MO.

Dining out

- *Dine out only for a reason.* We have become a nation of restaurant enthusiasts, some would even say addicts. Save eating out for special occasions and set a per week or per month limit on how often you'll leave your own kitchen at mealtime.

- *Drink at home.* Alcoholic beverages in a restaurant are always expensive. Invite friends to join you at home for cocktails and then go on to the restaurant.
- *Drink slowly.* If you enjoy cocktails or wine in a restaurant, order just one; if it's a group, order a carafe of the house wine or a pitcher of beer. Let the bottle of Verve Cliquot wait for the day you get a fat raise to cover its fat price.
- *Eat ethnic.* Mexican, Chinese, Thai, Japanese, Indian, and Pakistani restaurants are almost always a third less than American or Continental fare.
- *Skip the starter.* You'll save a quarter of the price of a meal if you bypass the appetizer. Ditto on the dessert—or share a dessert. You'll halve not only the price but the calories.
- *Look for specials.* If your lifestyle will accommodate it, take advantage of early bird specials, brunch, pretheater dinners, and prix fixe.
- *Order from the middle of the menu.* You don't have to eat the imported caviar, the filet mignon, the flaming dessert, and the exotic mixed drink.
- *Play accountant.* Always add up the check. Interestingly enough, most restaurant errors are in the restaurant's favor, not yours.
- *Take home leftovers.* Doggie bags are in. Some restaurants even mold their take-home foil packages into elegant shapes.

Discount Dining Cards

These companies give 20 to 30% off restaurant bills. You charge your meal using the card and then receive the discount on your monthly statement. Call to find out which card has the most restaurants in your area.

IGT (In Good Taste) 800-444-8872.

Transmedia 800-422-5090.

Travel World Leisure Club 800-444-8952; 212-239-4855.

LeCard 800-234-6377.

Premier Dining 800-346-3241.

Grocery shopping

It's easy to spend twice as much as you thought you would at the grocery store. You have to eat, but you can eat more reasonably with a little preplanning. So, before pushing the cart down the aisles again, read these 16 tips.

1. Never shop for groceries when you're hungry.
2. Always shop with a list—and stick to it.
3. Comparison shop and read the ads. Not all supermarkets charge the same price for the same items.
4. Shop only once or twice a week. This will force you to be organized and plan your meals.
5. Buy generic items—or at least give them a try.
6. Buy in bulk—if you'll use the items.
7. Join a food co-op (or start one). Discounts can be anywhere from 5 to 20% because items are packaged in bulk.
8. Shop at food warehouses; they usually have lower prices than supermarkets.
9. Shop on triple coupon days.
10. Steer clear of convenience stores unless it's midnight and an emergency. Prices are ridiculously high on most items.
11. Don't buy "pre" anything—that means precut, prepared, prechopped, presliced, prepackaged—if it's not necessary.

12. Buy soft drinks in large containers. If you get drinks from a vending machine at work, fill a thermos at home and take it with you. You'll save anywhere from 65 cents to $1.25/can.

13. Check unit prices, especially on single-serving items. They're amazingly expensive.

14. Read: *Leftovers: 200 Recipes* by Kathy Gunst, HarperCollins, 1991, $14.

15. Cook meals on weekends and freeze them in the right amount for individual or family dinners. Be certain to date and label each package so you don't wind up with two-year-old mystery items in your freezer.

16. Grow your own herbs. You can do this on your windowsill or terrace if you're not privy to several acres of farmland.

Generic
Any product (food, drug, cosmetic) that can be sold without a brand name; a product not protected by a trademark or registration.

Coupon Clipping
During the 1990s, Americans have been redeeming over 7 billion coupons worth $4 billion each year. The average face value of a coupon is 58 cents. Breakfast cereals offer the most coupons, followed by laundry detergents.

Buying clothes

Clothes may or may not make a man or woman, but they are fun and, of course, an obvious necessity. Unless you're a latter-day hippy, you feel good when you look your best—at work, when you go out for dinner, or to a party, or even when jogging or playing tennis. It's possible to dress extremely well without going overboard and spending a fortune. But it takes some time, effort, and a little imagination. It will help keep the price tag down when you shop if you bear in mind what one wit said about fashion: "It's something that goes out of style as soon as most people have one." Nor do you need a closet bulging with clothes—as my mother said, "you've only got one back on which to hang them." So, buy classic clothes that last from one season to the next and update with accessories—shoes, belts, scarves, neckties, shirts.

The obvious way to save is to shop at the sales—but the biggest bargains in clothes, especially good ones, are usually found at discount stores, outlets, off-price chains, and good quality second hand thrift shops. Some catalogs also offer clothing at a discount, but check shipping costs first—they can mount up quickly. Regardless of where you shop, assign a dollar amount to how much you'll spend and come home before you've reached it. A few more savings tips:

1. *Buy off season.*
2. *Buy suits with two pairs of pants.* Pants inevitably wear out first.
3. *Find a good tailor* to keep your clothes looking up to date and in good shape.
4. *Do your own ironing and button-sewing.*
5. *Finally, don't overlook upmarket thrift shops.* True fashion plates, celebrities, and party people think nothing of getting rid of designer outfits after several wearings, donating them to their pet charity for a tax deduction.

Mail Order Discounts

Save on gasoline or bus fare by shopping from home and get as much as 50% off.

Chadwick's of Boston
1 Chadwick Place
Box 1600
Brockton, MA 02403
508-583-6600

Women's clothing and accessories

Lee-McClain Co.
1857 Midland Trail
Shelbyville, KY 40065
502-633-3823

Men's suits and jackets

L'eggs Hanes Bali
Playtex
Box 748
Rural Hall, NC 27098
919-744-1790

Women's hosiery and underwear

Okum Brothers Shoes
356 East South Street
Kalamazoo, MI 49007
800-433-6344

Shoes for men and women

Nine Outlets

These and other outlets give discounts of 30% or more on clothes, accessories, shoes, toys, kitchen items.

Howland Place
651 Orchard Street
New Bedford, MA 02744
508-999-4100

Outlets at the Cove
45 Meadowlands Parkway
Secaucus, NJ 07094
201-392-8700

Potomac Mills
2700 Potomac Mills Circle
Prince William, VA 22192
800-VA-MILLS

Desert Hills Factory Stores
48650 Seminole Road
Cabazon, CA 92230
909-849-6641

Espirit Direct
16th and Illinois Streets
San Francisco, CA 94107
415-957-2540

Medford Outlet Center
315 County Road #12 SW
Medford, MN 55049
507-455-4111

San Marcos Factory Shops
3939 I-35 South
San Marcos, TX 78666
512-396-2200

Silverthorne Factory Stores
145 Stephenson Way
Silverthorne, CO 80498
303-468-9440

Freeport Merchant's Assn.
10 Morse Street
Freeport, ME 04032
207-865-1212

Outlet Guides

> *OUTLETBOUND: Guide to the Nation's Best Outlets* (Outlet Marketing Group, $6.95 plus $1.50 shipping; 800-336-8853). Matches manufacturer's name with outlets; includes 9,000 factory-direct stores and 300 outlet centers.
>
> *The Joy of Outlet Shopping* (Value Retail News, $5.95 plus $1.50 shipping; 800-344-6397). Inside scoop on 9,000 outlet stores and 325 outlet centers plus $200 worth of coupons.

Purchasing household items

A relatively new shopping concept, the no-frills warehouse, usually located on the edge of town, has rock-bottom prices. Most are open only to members who pay a yearly fee. The two leaders are the Price Costco

Club (800-597-7423) and Sam's Club, owned by Wal-Mart (800-444-2582). They sell food, office supplies, and other items at 8 to 10% above the wholesale cost.

Two other discount warehouses to find out about in your area: IKEA (215-834-0180) for home furnishings (in its 13 stores, you can drop off your kids in a free supervised play area while you shop) and Staples (800-333-3330) for office supplies.

You can also find an amazing amount of good furniture, even valuable antiques, at second-hand stores, house sales, garage sales, and auctions. Set aside some weekend time and look before you rush to a furniture or department store to buy new. The U.S. government also sells surplus goods and items seized in bankruptcies and other situations. You may have seen ads for books saying they have the inside info on great deals in government surplus. Don't waste your money. Everything you need to know, whether you're interested in a repossessed house or a used computer, is in the *U.S. General Services Administration Guide to Federal Government Sales*. For a free copy, send your name and address to: Federal Sales Guide, Pueblo, CO 81009.

Product warranties

No matter how carefully one shops, it's inevitable that eventually we wind up with something that doesn't work. To protect yourself, save receipts for all your major purchases and put them in a file folder marked "Products/Appliances." If you ever have a problem with something you've purchased or had repaired and it still is faulty, you'll need this documentation. Fill out and send in all warranty forms within two to three days of purchase. Then, put the owner's manual in your products file, along with your receipts.

Holiday and
Celebratory Occasions

'Tis the season to be jolly—but jolly often turns into foolish, with people going overboard on Christmas and Hanakuh gifts. The same temptations present themselves when a friend has a birthday, an anniversary, a new baby, or gets married. If you read the opening section of this chapter, you will have already budgeted a certain amount for gifts. Yet sometimes it seems as though all your friends are getting married or having babies at the same time. You may be asked to be in one or two weddings, which means extra expenses for special clothes, partying, and presents. If you find you are stretched to the max, one way to cut costs and still participate in all the fun is to give a personally made present. It is, in many ways, far more meaningful than buying another crystal vase, toaster oven, or set of place mats. Some ideas:

- Put together a photo album or scrapbook of your friend's life. Add amusing captions and dates. You can also do this for a relative's birthday. Plan far enough in advance that you can ask others to contribute snapshots or memorabilia.

- Do a painting of your friend or relative, his house, baby, dog, or cat and have it framed. Or, do the same with a handsome photo.

- Sew, knit, needlepoint, carve, or sculpt a present.

- Bake cookies, a cake, or make a special dish to augment a modestly priced purchased present.

- Treat your friend to a picnic or dinner for which you do all the preparation.

- Write a poem or story commemorating the event. Have it written in calligraphy, bound together or framed.

Some other ways to handle celebratory expenses:

- Sign up for the holiday savings plan at your bank; but only if you get interest on your deposits. A little hokey, but great for those who need help saving.
- Give savings bonds to newlyweds, babies, and young children. The minimum is only $25 and there's no purchase fee.
- Cut back on your Christmas card list. Make your own or send holiday postcards—the stamp is only 19 cents.
- Buy gifts when they are on sale.
- Buy wrapping paper and cards right after Christmas when they go on sale. You can count on there being another Christmas next year.

Savings Tips Your Mother Told You About But You Didn't Listen To Because She And/Or Your Dad Were Still Supporting You

- *Don't kid yourself, buying on sale* isn't saving, it's spending.
- *Just because you're going shopping* doesn't mean you have to come home with something.
- *Wait*—they'll mark it down.
- *Wait a little longer*—you'll see, you don't need it.
- *There's absolutely nothing wrong* with buying a floor model. Your uncle does it all the time.
- *Save your coins* at the end of the day. (An update: As Howard Hughes said, "A million dollars is not what it used to be." So aim to save quarters, not pennies.) Emptying your pockets at the end of the

day (and leaving the next day with empty pockets) can net you $200–$400 per year in small change.

- *Take it back!* Anyone can see: a) it doesn't work; b) it makes you look too fat/thin; c) it isn't "you"; or, d) your father wouldn't let you out of the house in that. So, be a grownup and get your money back when you make a mistake as a consumer.

And, had these spending possibilities been around when you were a kid, she would have added:

- *Don't use* overnight express service; we can't afford it.

Finally, you probably heard your parents say (and you'll probably say the same to your children):

- *I don't care if everyone else in school has one.* You don't need one.
- *We're not going to keep up with the Joneses.* As a kid, you may not have lived even remotely near any Joneses, but hundreds of them were so busy setting the pace in their neighborhoods they were unable to keep up with their own bills and were among the one million Americans that declare personal bankruptcy each year.

29 Ways To Boost Your Income

Even if you devise and follow the perfect budget, you may still need (or want) more money. In addition to lobbying for a raise or landing a higher-paying job, you can increase your income through a little creative moonlighting. Almost any skill can turn into a money-maker, so tap into your special talents. Then set up your own self-employment retirement plan—

either a Keogh or SEP (Simplified Employee Pension Plan). You can do this even if you have a retirement plan where you work. The money you put into a Keogh or SEP is tax deductible going in and grows on a tax-deferred basis until you take it out.

Moonlighting Ideas

Typing/word processing
Repairs/odd jobs
Cooking/catering
Writing/editing
Proofreading
Research
Sewing/alterations
Tutoring
Organizing parties
Run house/garage sales
Garden/yard work
Cleaning
Dog walking
Pet sitting
Painting/wallpapering
House sitting
Child care/babysitting
Calligraphy
Clipping service
Notary public
Secretarial work
Delivery service
Teaching weekends/evenings
Bookkeeping/tax preparation
Companion to elderly or shut-in
Chauffeur or taxi service

Three more instant income-boosters.
You can also get a part-time or weekend job, take in a paying roommate or boarder, or rent out your apartment, house, or garage when you're not using them.

PART FIVE

Your Personal Life

The little orgies in your life may result in living with someone, getting married, even having a baby; or perhaps having a sumptuous dinner party or going on a great vacation.

"Life: Routine punctuated by little orgies."

Aldous Huxley

12 *Live-Togethers & Newlyweds*

This definition also could be said to apply to living together. In either case, whether you run around in T-shirts and cut-offs or silk dressing gowns, you'll be dealing with money: yours, as well as his or hers. It can be sticky unless you talk about it.

Money is an important ingredient in your personal life, whether you're living with someone, married or divorced. Despite its importance, it's tempting to put off financial planning because it seems so unromantic—reducing love to dollars, cents and percentages. Yet having a well designed plan will not only help you and those you live with take control of your financial well being, it also helps prevent unpleasant surprises. And, should your relationship eventually come to an end, you will be able to make your exit on a friendlier note and with fewer complications and less financial havoc.

When Dad brought home the bacon and Mom cooked it, managing money for couples was relatively easy. But today deciding who pays for what, who writes the checks and who determines how much to

"Marriage: Paying an endless visit in your worst clothes"

J.B. Priestly

spend on vacations is no more on automatic pilot. Add to that the fact that people live together in a myriad of ways—in couples, in groups, as straight, as gay, as married, as unmarried, as common law, as friends— there are no uniform answers that apply to everyone. However, sensible strategies that put you and your partner or mate on sound financial footing do exist.

To begin with, you need to be open and work hard not to let the lines of communication break down when it comes to money. If you feel you can't be honest with the person with whom you're sharing shelter, then perhaps you shouldn't be together in the first place. You also need to be flexible; any financial program, like any diet, that is too rigid will collapse before very long.

You can further ensure financial bliss, whether you're living together or married, by setting up three things: your goals, a budget and an agreement— preferably a written agreement. Although it was sort of okay for you to muddle along, haphazardly balancing your checkbook or saving on a hit or miss basis when you were flying solo, such poor money habits can create serious problems with the person you've chosen to live with.

Regardless of your status, take time to read this entire chapter. Even though you may be a live-together and not a married, or vice versa, you will encounter suggestions for both categories that can be adapted to your particular situation quite easily. And, during the course of your life, you may very well move from one category to another and back again.

Live-Togethers

If you're sharing living space with a legally unrelated friend or lover, openness and a written policy are the two ingredients most likely to guarantee a successful financial relationship and to keep complications to a minimum.

Preprinted Couples Agreements
- "The Living Together Kit; A Detailed Guide to Help Unmarried Couples Deal With Legal Realities" by Toni Ihara & Ralph Warner
  Nolo Press
  950 Parker Street
  Berkeley, CA 94710; $17.95

It's also important to keep in mind from the very beginning that live-togethers have far fewer rights than married couples. While local laws vary, married couples who divorce generally have a right to an equitable share of the property acquired during the marriage, whereas unmarried mates are typically entitled only to assets held in their own name.

When you live with someone else, financial problems are seldom very evident at the start—it's a happy and exciting time in your life. But if the relationship starts to get sticky or unwind, you may suddenly find yourself fighting over things you thought were yours—the Victorian writing desk, the motorcycle, the juicer, the sofa bed—because you bought them with your own money. You can reduce such wrangling by using a little common sense at the very beginning.

A Primer for Unmarried Partners

Here are eight ways to handle the unique financial situations that live togethers face.

1. Establish the ground rules in advance. The simplest arrangements are those where you both earn approximately the same salary, split ex-

penses down the middle, and then pay for your own individual "extras" of special things—your exercise class, long distance calls, your football tickets. Handle major bills, such as the rent and utilities, by writing separate but equal checks.

Of course it's not always that simple. We all bring old feelings about money to new situations and the 50–50 plan is trickier if you and your friend don't have roughly equal incomes. Then devise an appropriate percentage approach: if you earn one-third more, then you pay one-third more. If one of you feels this is unfair, the person with less income can contribute in other ways—clean-up detail, grocery shopping, keeping the household records, writing checks, child care, etc.

2. Have individual as well as joint financial goals. Don't lose sight of your personal aims simply because you're now living with someone else.

3. Keep separate credit and charge cards. If you authorize another person to use your American Express, Visa or MasterCard, you are responsible for all purchases made and could wind up with a ruined credit rating through no fault of your own.

 If your partner earns more than you, don't take advantage of the situation by using his or her credit cards. If you don't have enough income to pay for it yourself, you probably shouldn't be buying it.

4. Put both names on the lease if you are renting.

5. Make certain that your renter's or homeowner's insurance policy lists both your names, regardless of who signed the lease or who owns the

house. And, don't tell the insurance company you're married if you're not: such fraud could invalidate your policy just when you go to collect.

6. Have a buy-sell agreement. If you decide to purchase a house, this agreement says that before the house is sold, either of you has the chance to buy out the other's share.

7. Keep checking and savings accounts in your name. Joint checking accounts mean you are responsible for any checks either one of you writes. Joint savings gives each of you the right to withdraw all the money. Instead, save, but in two separate accounts. As an alternative, you might want to maintain a joint checking account to pay for joint living expenses.

8. Avoid making one-time big-ticket purchases jointly. Color TV's and Bokhara rugs can't be split in half. If you decide you need a dishwasher, one person should purchase it, keeping a record in case you part ways.

Buying Property Together

Owning together can be a very financially savvy move. It enables those who can't afford to buy a house on their own to become property owners. Yet, many unmarried adults team up to buy condos and homes together, sealing the deal with a kiss and glass of champagne only to discover later on that without a contract, legal and financial hassles can ruin everything.

Before the celebrated California "palimony" decision in 1976 involving actor Lee Marvin and his live-in companion, courts in most states did not enforce written contracts between live-togethers. But since then, heterosexual and homosexual live-togethers with written contracts have often received money and property after splitting up. Of course, a written contract can be challenged, but it also can provide some protection. Without it, it's your word against your partner's.

Of course, anticipating breaking up is not the only reason to have a written agreement. It also enables you to focus on how you will manage day to day, making the most out of what you both earn. You can use a prepared fill-in agreement (see sidebar) or draw one up with the advice of a lawyer.

WHEN IN DOUBT, SPELL IT OUT

Once you own real estate you absolutely need a contract to protect your rights—after all, that person you co-own the condo with might be transferred or get married, or if the two of you are romantically linked and the romance fades, you'll need solid protection.

The points to put in writing, with the help of a lawyer, are:

1. How will the mortgage and down payments be divided?
2. What will the arrangements be for sharing the cost or running the house after moving in—maintenance, repairs, utilities, etc.?
3. What form of title will be used?
4. Who may pay to live on the property besides the parties originally involved in the deal and for what length of time? Can one partner sublease to someone else?
5. What will you do about mortgage payments if one becomes seriously ill, loses a job or moves?
6. If one partner invests more than the other, how

will the unequal interests be taken into consideration when the property is sold?

7. What is the plan if one person decides to move out? Does the second owner have the right to buy out the first? If so, at what price? Can the first owner sell his share to another person without veto power by the second owner?

8. How will possessions be disposed of if one owner dies?

9. How will payment defaults be handled? Often it is agreed that if one party cannot meet his share of the payments temporarily, the other will cover them for a certain time length, planning to be repaid with interest.

10. What arrangements have been made for non-paying persons to live with you? Can one of the owners bring in a friend and if so how much will that person pay? How long can guests remain? Are children allowed?

11. What method will be used for handling arguments: separate lawyers, a common lawyer, or according to who has the most invested in the property?

Your lawyer will help you address all of these issues, but you will have a better agreement if you have thought about some of the solutions beforehand. For example, one lawyer came up with this ingenious answer to resolving deadlocks—he had it written into the partnership agreement that the cost of an arbitrator for unresolved conflicts between the partners would be billed at $1,000 a day.

Your best move, unless your lawyer advises otherwise, is to hold title to your property as "tenancy in common." Then, if either dies, the other's share will pass to his or her estate instead of to the co-owner. On the other hand, if your relationship becomes long-term, you may want to change it to joint tenants so the survivor will inherit the late co-owner's share.

Another modification—hold the property as tenants in common but stipulate that if one dies the other has the right to remain in the home as long as he or she lives. Then, take out an insurance policy on the other so that the survivor would have cash from the policy to pay off half of the mortgage, leaving the survivor with the same monthly mortgage payment as before.

One way to handle financial problems is to stipulate that if the other owner doesn't pay his share of mortgage, repair, maintenance and utility costs, he forfeits the right to live in the house or condo, or failure to make payments could be offset against sale proceeds at some future date.

Stipulate a procedure for one co-owner to sell out. If you can't agree on a price, hire an appraiser. If each of you hires an appraiser and their figures differ, the contract can require you to average the two figures, or to hire a third appraiser who will make a binding appraisal.

If You're Gay

About 25 cities, counties and states allow unmarried couples to register as domestic partners. Such registration provides only limited benefits and rights, such as extended unpaid maternity leaves and tenancy rights in rent-regulated housing.

In recent years, however, more and more employers, often in the nonprofit sector, have begun offering the live-in partner of unmarried workers the same health care and employee benefits available to spouses and children.

At first, keep it separate, simple and equal:

- maintain individual checking and savings accounts
- maintain individual credit cards
- put both names on your apartment lease
- put both names on renter's insurance policy
- share expenses

Then, have a written agreement if:

- you purchase real estate together
- you purchase big ticket items together

Be sure to:

- describe items purchased, date purchased and how much each contributed
- keep receipts and canceled checks
- outline responsibilities for mortgage or any other payments (on a car, for example)
- specify who gets which items in the event of splitting up or death

Prenuptial Agreements

The divorce between Donald and Ivana Trump focused our attention on an increasingly common ingredient of marriage in the 1990s—the prenuptial agreement. Prenups are not just for billionaires like the Trumps. If you and your beloved/intended have raised the "M" word, you may also need to talk about the "P" word, especially if one of you is wealthier than the other, owns a business, has a trust fund or will inherit family assets. Even if you're not wealthy, you should think about one if you or your fiance have careers in which your incomes are expected to increase dramatically.

> **To Increase The Chances Of Your Prenup Standing Up In Court**
> * Prepare and sign it several months before the wedding
> * Have it notarized
> * Have both people disclose all assets and liabilities
> * Have separate attorneys
> * Describe the property to be transferred

The agreement defines the property each of you brings into the marriage and your financial intentions in case the marriage ends. It usually includes a transfer of some property to the less wealthy spouse in exchange for a release of any claims the less wealthy may have later on for support from or against the wealthier person's estate. Prenuptials can also protect the inheritances of children from a previous marriage as well as protect second wives from being responsible for a husband's alimony or child-support payments.

Prenupts tend to be legally binding if both parties are open and honest about their assets and both have access to legal advice—translation: each of you should have your own lawyer. Most states allow one spouse to limit his or her interest in the other spouse's estate but few allow contracts that absolutely limit or forbid alimony.

Once you have set a date for your wedding, plan to have the agreement signed; if it is signed too close to your marriage, a lawyer may argue later on that one or the other of you signed under duress. Of course, if you have a very long engagement like Octavio Guillen and Adriana Martinez, who finally took the plunge after 67 years in June 1969 in Mexico City, you'll need to check with your lawyer about updating the contract.

A His-And-Hers Monthly Budget

EXPENSES	WHO PAYS HOW MUCH?		
Fixed	*She*	*He*	*Total*
Rent or mortgage	$_____	$_____	$_____
Food	$_____	$_____	$_____
Utilities	$_____	$_____	$_____
Medical	$_____	$_____	$_____
Car loan	$_____	$_____	$_____
Credit card debt	$_____	$_____	$_____
Savings	$_____	$_____	$_____
Tuition	$_____	$_____	$_____
Commute to work	$_____	$_____	$_____
Other	$_____	$_____	$_____
GRAND TOTALS	$_____	$_____	$_____
Discretionary	*She*	*He*	*Total*
Clothing	$_____	$_____	$_____
Furniture	$_____	$_____	$_____
Entertainment	$_____	$_____	$_____
Vacations & travel	$_____	$_____	$_____
Presents	$_____	$_____	$_____
Liquor	$_____	$_____	$_____
Charitable contributions	$_____	$_____	$_____
Books, magazines, newspapers	$_____	$_____	$_____
Other	$_____	$_____	$_____
GRAND TOTALS	$_____	$_____	$_____

Married Couples

After the wedding gifts have been put away and the last thank-you note has been written, it's time to think about financial matters. Here we'll discuss money matters only as they are entwined with marriage. You'll soon discover, if you haven't already, that sharing your days and nights also means learning how to earn, save and spend money together. And, no matter how much you love each other you're bound to have disagreements. In fact, financial battles between couples predate the barter system and wampum and at no time are you more vulnerable than as newlyweds. And, most newlyweds, accustomed to making their own financial decisions, suddenly find themselves having to consult one another. Although you certainly don't need to agree on how every dollar is spent—in fact, part of your budget should be earmarked for individual goals, it is smart to set some basic ground rules early on—for example, not to spend more than $500 or $1,000 without discussing it first.

Read:
"Your Legal Guide To Marriage & Other Relationships"—$5.50 from:
    American Bar Association
    Order Department
    750 North Lake Shore Drive
    Chicago, IL 60611
    312-988-5522

Going From Pillow Talk to Money Talk

As women hit the fast track, break through the glass ceiling, juggle career, baby and house, earning and handling money is a natural part of their lives. Some earn more than their husbands. Men, on the other hand, take paternity leaves; some work at home. They may or may not make more than their wives. Here are some tips on how to make it all work:

- Discuss money matters; don't sweep them under the rug.
- Divide financial responsibilities.
- Have at least one joint account; it fosters the part-

nership. Use it to pay regular bills—rent, cleaning service, food, utilities, household expenses. Automatically transfer excess funds to a joint money market account with a higher interest rate. Use your money market account to pay large bills, your mortgage, and for your vacation and other nonessentials.

- Have separate accounts to cover those things you want to do on your own—to pay for clothes, dinner out with your buddies, your continuing education course, your exercise class, spa visit or white water rafting trip.

- Plan goals jointly—what's important to both of you—moving to a larger apartment, buying a house, going back to school, having a baby? Write them down with a time frame in which to achieve them attached.

- Get organized. Set up space for financial papers; buy a filing cabinet for records; pay bills and balance your checkbooks every month.

- Delegate and rotate. Take turns handling the financial paperwork so you both know what's going on and so you both will gain hands-on financial experience. Then, in the event of illness or if one of you must travel out of town regularly, or even if you must face death or divorce, you will be able to carry on intelligently.

- Hold a board meeting. Plan to really talk about your financial future at least twice a year—do it at a quiet restaurant, over coffee on a Saturday morning or some other time when you won't be interrupted. Review your joint and individual financial goals—are you meeting them? Do you need to save more money? Are you ready to make a down payment on a house? Deal with your financial matters as if you were solving a problem at work—intelligently, non-emotionally, and with a written list of objectives and a time schedule.

 Newlyweds should save 5% of their joint income, minimum. Aim for 20% within five years.

Resolving conflicts

Don't be surprised to discover that your spouse is more reckless with money than you realized, or a closet tightwad. Couples often have different money personalities—perhaps proving that the old phrase opposites attract is true. If you have lopsided money habits, turning all medium- and high-ticket purchases into joint decisions often helps resolve the issue. Yet take care that the focus is not on who is at fault, or who spends too much or is too penurious, but rather on the fact that it is important that both of you work together to keep spending within bounds, bounds that are acceptable to both of you.

> **Read:**
> "How To Stop Fighting About Money and Make Some"
>   by Adriane Berg
>   Avon Books, 1989, $4.50

Handling Hidden Debt

It can come as a great shock—you thought your spouse was financially sensible only to discover when you get back from the honeymoon and start paying bills that your mate is heavily into debt. It may merely be that he or she ran up credit card bills to cover wedding expenses. However, it's not a good sign and you need to discuss it carefully. Together, set up a program to pay down the debt.

If you're the one that brought debt to the marriage, it is time for you to assume responsibility for your fiscal behavior. Tell your husband or wife just how you will handle it and then do. It may be difficult for your spouse to completely trust or respect you until you settle the matter.

Turning to the Folks

Taking money from your parents can often ease the way, particularly if one of you is still in school, you are buying a house, or expecting a baby. But it can also lead to problems. If your family offers to give you money, talk it over with your spouse first. If you both agree to accept the offer, set up specific terms for paying back the money, even if it's very slowly and over a long period of time. Your parents may refuse to take your payments, but offer them anyway. Emotional independence is frequently linked to financial independence.

Handling an Inheritance

There are two ways to approach inheritance: one, that the money belongs solely to the person inheriting it and therefore can be used as that person wishes; or two, that you adhere to the "what's mine is yours" philosophy and jointly decide upon its use. There's no right or wrong way to manage inherited money or property, but you should treat it with great respect and perhaps divide its use—putting part into savings and part toward something wonderful that you wouldn't do otherwise.

When a Marriage Ends

Sometimes marriage simply doesn't work out. If yours is coming unglued, it's very important to make wise financial moves now so after you're divorced you will be able to live comfortably. Here are the key financial considerations; your lawyer will help you with the specifics.

Divorce laws basically maintain that husband and wife together own what's called "marital property." This includes everything earned, saved, and purchased by either one of you during the marriage, no matter whose name is on the deed or account. The exceptions to this are gifts and inheritances not put into a joint account and the original value of assets obtained before you were married.

Alimony is now largely a thing of the past. Most no-fault divorce laws view a husband and wife as economic partners, so that if the marriage ends, it is assumed that the woman can support herself by working. Exception: temporary spousal maintenance sometimes is given to help an ex-wife make the transition to being self-supporting.

Usually, although not always, the ex-wife gets custody of the children, the house and the mortgage.

Protecting Yourself

You can protect yourself financially by doing your homework. Your lawyer will want copies of brokerage and mutual fund statements, joint income-tax returns, pension or profit-sharing plans, a list of safe deposit box contents and information about your spouse's company perks and insurance policies.

- Start putting savings in an account in your name. Then you'll have cash on hand for expenses if your spouse stops contributing money.
- Make an inventory of all jointly and separately owned assets, including cars, property, investments, furniture. Add to it a list of outstanding debts. Have your bank verify the content of any joint safe deposit box.

- Notify banks and brokerage firms where you had joint accounts that you are getting divorced. Close joint charge accounts and notify creditors in writing that you will no longer be responsible for your spouse or ex-spouse's purchases. Keep copies and have proof of the notification.
- After the divorce decree becomes final, rewrite your will and change beneficiaries on insurance policies and retirement plans.

For Women Only

If you are a woman, take these immediate steps to become less financially vulnerable:

- Have a bank account in your own name
- Have credit cards in your own name so you can establish your own credit rating
- Have a record of detailed monthly expenses to know what it costs to support the family
- Do not move out of the house unless you're in an abusive or otherwise intolerable situation. Leaving seriously weakens your claim on it and if there are children at home, leaving could also damage your claim to custody.

What Is Marital Property?

- Savings and checking accounts, CDs
- Stocks, bonds, options, commodity contracts, mutual funds
- Other sources of income, rents, royalties, trusts, partnerships
- Usually a business acquired during the marriage
- Mortgages, car loans, personal loans
- Credit card debts
- Life insurance, annuities
- Pensions and profit-sharing plans

- Professional licenses (medical, legal) obtained and practices established during the marriage
- Appreciation of assets during the marriage that were obtained before the marriage
- Real estate, household furnishings, cars, boats, motorcycles
- Jewelry, art, antiques, collectibles, valuables

13 And Baby Makes Three: When You Become the Parent

With your baby's arrival, your money-making ability will need to not only go on, but will need to go up, as children are an expensive proposition.

So, as soon as you (or your spouse or friend) know you're expecting you'll need to begin making financial decisions that take a third person into consideration. And once you receive the obstetrician's bill, you'll know that bringing up baby is going to be as much about dollars and cents as it is about ABCs and day care.

Here's a parents' checklist of financial considerations for the baby's first year:

- Find out what your employers offer in terms of health care, maternity and paternity leave.
- Start saving money right away, stashing all or part of one of your salaries in a money market fund.
- Live on one salary, which you'll be doing when one of you takes time off from work to have the baby.

"A baby is God's opinion that the world should go on."

Carl Sandberg

- Divide your nest egg into two categories: put half into a money market fund so you can draw on it to pay immediate bills when the baby arrives. Put the other half into a revolving certificate of deposit program, purchasing CDs with staggered maturity dates so you'll have regular extra income during this expensive time of life.
- Save to decorate a room for the baby, add on a nursery or even buy a house.
- Buy life insurance—you'll need to get serious now about coverage, especially if you buy a house as well as have a child. Provide enough for the surviving spouse to continue making mortgage payments or pay off the loan, to run the household and educate your baby.
- Name your child as a contingent beneficiary on any group life insurance or pension plan.
- Add the baby to your health coverage—you have 30 days from the date of birth to do it without providing medical insurability.
- Review your fringe benefits. If your employer offers a cafeteria-style benefits plan, you should rethink the package. Take advantage of a dependent-care reimbursement account, for instance.

- Name a guardian. Both of you will need a will to name a guardian for your child. Your will also determines how your assets are to be distributed.

- Talk to your lawyer about a durable power of attorney, naming your spouse to act as your agent should you become incapacitated.

- Get your child a Social Security number so he can be claimed as a dependent. Most hospitals arrange to have a number given out at birth. But make certain. Call the Social Security Administration, 800-772-1213 to get the ball rolling. No bank or brokerage firm will open an account for anyone without a Social Security number.

- Set up a college fund. Cash gifts can be put into a savings account. However by law, children cannot own securities directly. Most parents set up a custodial account for their child. They come in two flavors: a Uniform Gift to Minors Act account or a Uniform Transfers to Minors Account. State laws dictate which type can be used. They can be opened with stockbrokers, banks and mutual funds. The custodian manages the account with the child's best interest in mind until the child reaches age 18 or 21, when he can take control of the account. (An accountant can tell you about other types of accounts for children.)

And Baby Makes Three: When You Become the Parent   **231**

> **Custodian**
> A bank or other financial institution that keeps custody of stock certificates and other assets of an individual, mutual fund or corporate client.

1. As long as your child is under the age of 14 and his unearned income is $600 or less, he is not required to pay tax on that income.

2. If your child's unearned income is between $601 and $1,200, he or she will be taxed at his rate on that money. (A child's rate is usually 15%).

3. If the child has more than $1,200 of unearned income, he or she will be taxed at your rate, which will most likely be higher than your child's rate.

4. If the child has earned income, that amount will be taxed at the child's rate.

5. For kids 14 and older, all income, unearned or earned, will be taxed at the child's rate, again usually 15%.

> **Unearned Income**
> This income is derived from investments, not from paid work or employment.

Savings Tips

There are lots of common sense ways to save money with a baby. The popular parent/child magazines are filled with tips. A few to get you started:

- Say yes to all baby showers.

- Borrow maternity clothes, baby clothes as well as equipment from friends, or buy from second hand shops, discount stores and outlets.

- Form a babysitting co-op.
- Don't be lured into buying expensive designer clothes, toys and equipment—your baby doesn't know whether he's riding in a pram or a carriage.
- Try working at home and hiring a student sitter rather than a professional.

14 *The Flip Side of Working: Fun*

"All work
and no
play makes
Jack a dull
boy."

Anon.

Finding Fun Money

You may be so busy moving up the career ladder that
there seems to be no time-out for the fun side of life.
Or, you may think that playing, traveling and entertaining are too expensive and will keep you from becoming financially secure. But the good life on the
cheap is easy and painless provided you're armed with
inside information and a good budget. This *A-TO-Z
GUIDE* is packed with over 50 money-saving ideas in
these categories: Airline travel, Camping, Family
travel, Health and fitness, Learning vacations, Lodging, Money matters, Solo Travel, Parties, Trips and
tours, and Volunteer vacations.

Before engaging in any of these ideas, draw up a
budget and make every effort to stick to it, using the
worksheets below.

Playing Near Home

At least once a year you should treat yourself to some time off from work or school. First some general tips for playing within your budget:

1. *Go local.* Your high school or college baseball, hockey, football and basketball games are cheaper than professional sporting events. Take your own lunch and snacks.
2. *Play locally.* Sign up for your local (or company's) sports teams.
3. *Jog* with pals.
4. *Check your newspaper* for list of free concerts and events. Plan a picnic or party around them.
5. *Join* your local YMCA or YWCA. The price is right and less than a private health club or gym.

Traveling

1. *Leave all but one credit card at home* and it should have a spending cap. Take plenty of traveler's checks. Then you'll think twice about buying something you don't need.
2. *Stay* at budget motels, youth hostels, campus dorms, YMCAs, and with family, friends.
3. *Eat in coffee shops* (but not those in hotels; they're outrageously pricey), museum cafes, university cafeterias and places where you can bring your own bottle of wine.
4. *Go* camping, fishing, or houseboating. Check with the houseboat Assn. of America, 4940 N. Rhett Avenue, Charleston, SC 29405; 803-744-6581.
5. *Drive* someone else's car and get there for free. Check your telephone book under "Automobile Transporters and Drive Away Companies," the classified ads in the newspaper and your bulletin board at work or school.

Vacation/Travel Budget

To control spending, fill out this worksheet *before* purchasing tickets or making a deposit.

Total Amount I Can Afford	$_____
Airline, train, bus tickets	$_____
Bus/taxi to airport/train station	$_____
Car rental	$_____
My car costs (gas, oil, tolls)	$_____
Lodging cost (per night: $_____) Total:	$_____
Food (per day: $_____) Total:	$_____
Tickets to theater, museums, sites	$_____
Fees (parking, campsites, etc)	$_____
Telephone calls home/ to office	$_____
Souvenirs and gifts	$_____
Vaccinations/medical supplies	$_____
Equipment rental/purchase	$_____
Tips and taxes	$_____
Kids' allowance	$_____

Steps:

1. Determine the total amount first.
2. If you're taking a tour or packaged trip, find out if the price includes meals, all transportation, tips, taxes.
3. Then enter dollar amounts into appropriate categories.
4. If you're over your budget, reduce spending for gifts or souvenirs, get a friend to drive you to the airport, and/or cut the length of your vacation.

Air Travel

BE A COURIER

If you can leave pretty much at the last minute and manage with only carry-on luggage, you can fly abroad for half or more off the usual fare as a courier. Although you're delivering something for someone else, heavy lifting is not part of the deal—couriers carry a list of the items being shipped under their name but typically never see the cargo. Your luggage allotment is given to the courier firm. The best way to find about tickets is through one of the booking agencies that link courier companies with passengers.

- Now Voyager, 212-431-1616
- Discount Travel International, 212-362-3636
- Halbart Express, 718-656-8279
- Polo Express, 415-742-9613
- Way-To-Go Travel, 213-466-1126

The International Association of Air Travel Couriers in Lake Worth, FL publishes a courier newsletter and price sheet ($35/year for membership). 407-582-8320.

More About Couriers
"The Insiders Guide to Air Courier Bargains" by Kelly Monaghan; The Intrepid Traveler, 1994, Upper Access Books, $14.95; 800-356-9315.

Camping

CAMP IN OUR STATE AND NATIONAL PARKS

It's fairly inexpensive, but reserve early as the best parks fill up quickly in the spring and summer. Then, take park tours, which are free or inexpensive. Call the Department of the Interior for locations, 703-358-1744.

GO BACK TO CAMP

And take along your parents, sisters, brothers and kids. Many summer camps have programs for the whole family—swimming, riflery, horseback riding, hiking, arts, crafts, softball, etc. In addition to the low cost, no one will squabble over who will set the table, cook or clean. Some suggestions:

- Burbank Family YMCA Camp Earl-Ana, Tehachapi, CA. 818-845-8551
- Camp Friendship, near Charlottesville, VA. 800-873-3223
- Camp Lincoln/Camp Lake Hubert, Brainard, MN. 800-242-1909

- Camp Mishawaka, Grand Rapids, MI, 218-326-5011
- Cheley Colorado Camp, 75 miles northwest of Denver, Estes Park, CO. 303-377-3616
- Montecito-Sequoia Lodge, between Sequoia and King Canyon national parks, CA. 800-227-9900
- YMCA Camp Flaming Arrow, on the Guadalupe River, near Hunt, TX. 215-238-4631
- YMCA of the Ozarks, 70 miles south of St. Louis, MO. 314-438-2154.

Family Fun

Some special places beckon families year after year because they have a wide range of activities, a friendly owner, and a well designed children's program.

PICK A RESORT FOR ALL AGES

These eight places have activities for everyone, from toddlers to grandparents and most offer babysitting and child care.

- Balsams Grand Resort Hotel in Dixville, NH; 800-255-0600; in NH: 800-255-0800. Bermuda in the White Mountains with all activities.
- La Casa Del Zorro in Borrego Springs, CA; 800-824-1884; 619-767-5323. Two and three-bedroom *casitas* in the Anza Borrego Desert, one of the largest state parks in the continental U.S.
- Tides Lodge in Irvington, VA; 800-248-4337. Small, family-run, bounded on three sides by water; two hours from the Chesapeake Bay.

The Flip Side of Working: Fun

- Dillman's Sand Lake Lodge in Lac du Flambeau, WI; 715-588-3143. A cabin resort on a sand-bottom lake.
- Nelson's Resort in Crane Lake, MN 218-993-2295. Rustic cabins surrounded by US national forest with 40 miles of continuous water-ways.
- Smugglers' Notch in Smugglers' Notch, VT; 800-451-8752. Flanked by three mountains, good in summer or winter; has a well known kids' camp.
- El Rancho Stevens in Gaylord, MI; 517-732-5090. A guest ranch for all ages with hayrides, cookouts, square dancing.
- Rocking Horse Ranch in Highland, NY; 800-647-2624. Hudson Valley ranch/resort 90 minutes from Manhattan.

Sleeping on the Road

There's no reason to spend a fortune on a place to sleep. You'll have just as much fun trying one of these more off-beat places.

BED & BREAKFAST

Although you may wind up sharing a bathroom, B&B's are a whole lot less pricey and much friendlier than hotels. Even if you're going to a big city, check them out. In New York, for example, you can book a loft, a room with bath in an apartment, or a town house through City Lights B&B, 212-737-7049. For nationwide listing of B&B's, send a self-addressed, stamped envelope to:

Complete Guide to B&Bs
    Box 20467
    Oakland, CA 94620

STAY IN A UNIVERSITY DORM

This is a great way to slash the cost of putting your head on the pillow. For example, a room at Catholic University in Washington, DC is $18/night and one on the 250-acre Goddard College estate in Vermont is $15/night. For a list of 600 of these inexpensive havens, consult "The U.S. and Worldwide Travel Accommodations. Guide." It covers universities in the US, Canada, Europe, New Zealand and Australia. Rooms range from $18 to $35/night. Campus Travel Service, Box 5486, Fullerton, CA 92635; $14 for book rate ($1.50 extra for first class mail), 800-525-6633; 714-525-6625.

STAY IN A RETREAT CENTER

For example, you can unwind at California's Colonial Mission Retreat for $37/night, including three meals, use of a swimming pool and spa. For a description of 450 inexpensive havens, consult: "Guide To Retreat Centers and Guest Houses," CTS Publications, Box 8335, Newport Beach, CA 92660, $14.95; 714-720-3729.

Youth hostels
The "American Youth Hostel Handbook," which lists over 300 US and Canadian hostels, is free to members and $8 to non-members. Info: American Youth Hostels, Inc., Box 37613, Washington, DC 20013.

> **YMCA Lodgings**
> Room rates range from $18 to $85/night. For a list of US and foreign accommodations, send a legal sized envelope with 65 cents postage to:
>
> Y's Way International
>   224 East 47th Street
>   New York, NY 10017
>   212-308-2899

ALWAYS GET A HOTEL DISCOUNT

By using special booking agencies you'll get up to 60% off hotel rooms in most U.S. cities. There's no charge for the service.

- Accommodations Express, 800-444-7666, 609-645-8688
- Capitol Reservations (Washington, DC area) 800-847-4832
- Central Reservation Service, 800-950-0232
- Express Hotel Reservations (Los Angeles & New York) 800-356-1123
- San Francisco Reservations, 800-677-1550, 415-227-1500

TRY A EUROPEAN HOMESTAY

Board with local families—it not only sets you apart from mere tourists, but you get to know the people and prices are far less than in hotels.

"Home From Home" lists programs in 50 countries. Published by The Central Bureau for Educational Visits and Exchanges of London; distributed by Seven Hills, 513-381-3881; $14.95 plus $2.00 shipping.

The major expense of traveling is lodging; here's a way to reduce it to nearly zip. Get listed with one of these home swapping agencies at least six months in advance. Contact the following ones for info about membership fees and other details.

- Vacation Exchange Club 800-638-3841
- Intervac Home Exchange 800-756-HOME
- Loan-A-Home 914-664-7640
- Worldwide Home Exchange 301-680-8950

Solo Travel

There are organizations and booking services geared specifically to single travelers. For example, Club Med (800-CLUB-MED) operates resorts and cruises for singles (and couples, too). Carnival Cruises (800-327-9501) has a singles plan that guarantees same-sex sharing of cabins to cut costs. Cunard Line's "Queen Elizabeth II" has a last minute standby fare; (800-221-4770). Singleworld (800-223-6490) buys blocks of staterooms on cruise ships and sells them to singles at reduced rates. Solo Flights (800-266-1566; 203-226-9993) organizes reasonably priced domestic and foreign trips for singles.

Trips & Tours

Join a club or association

Their outings and trips are almost always cheaper than commercial tours. Check your phone book for your local National Audubon Society, or call the head-quarters in New York, 212-979-3000, for the chapter nearest you.

Other organizations with inexpensive day trips include the Appalachian Mountain Club, 603-466-2721; The Sierra Club, 415-776-2211; the Adirondack Mountain Club, 518-668-4447; and the Nature Conservancy, 703-841-5300.

And, call your college or university; many alumni associations organize trips for grads.

TAKE A HIKE

Walking the road less traveled will get you in good condition and not cost an arm and a leg. Week-long trips are usually under $800; weekend trips, around $250. Some organizers:

- Hiking Holidays, Box 750 RF, Bristol, VT 05443; 802-453-4816
- River Odysseys West, Box 579, Coeur d'Alene, ID 83816; 800-451-6034
- Walking the World, Box 1186, Fort Collins, CO 80522; 303-225-0500
- Appalachian Mountain Club, Box 298, Gorham, NH 03581; 603-466-2727
- Glacier Wilderness Guides, Box 535, West Glacier, MT 59936; 800-521-RAFT

TAKE A BIKE

Whether it's an inn to inn journey, a bike and sail or bike and raft combo or a one day outing, there are trips to suit every level and every budget.

- Vermont Bicycle Touring, 802-453-4811
- Backroads Bicycle Touring, 800-245-3874
- American Youth Hostels, 202-783-6161.

Volunteer Vacations: Beyond the Suntan

DO SOME GOOD

Margaret Mead in her book put it well: " ... almost anything that really matters to us ... depends on some form ... of volunteerism." Volunteer vacations that take you to far corners of the world typically involve only travel expenses. And, you'll gain knowledge, experience and a sense of accomplishment. You may become involved in saving the endangered olive ridley sea turtle in Costa Rica, in helping people in rural areas of Africa, Asia and the South Pacific, build homes and community centers, or, closer to home, renovate schools along the Mississippi River.

Prices range from $300 to $400 for a week (excluding air fare) to $1,000+ for longer stays.

- Earthwatch, 680 Mount Auburn Street, Watertown, MA 02272; 617-926-8200
- Friendship Force, 57 Forsyth Street, NW, Atlanta, GA 30303; 800-688-6777
- Global Volunteers, 375 East Little Canada Road, St. Paul, MN 55117; 800-487-1074
- Habitat for Humanity, 121 Habitat Street, Americus, GA 31709; 912-924-6935
- Sierra Club Service Outings, 730 Polk Street, San Francisco, CA 94109; 415-776-2211
- University Research Expeditions Program, University of California, 2223 Fullerton, Berkeley, CA 94720; 510-642-6586

Appendix

Software That Makes Money Management a Snap

A personal computer can be a great tool for managing money, tracking your expenses, preparing your tax return—if the software matches your needs. Here are the top picks:

Checkbook Management

Microsoft Money. Great for keeping track of your checkbook and budget. Does calculations automatically.

Quicken. Easy to learn and use. Sorts financial info into budget and tax categories for record-keeping.

Financial Planning

Moneycounts. A flexible program that handles cash, checking, savings, investments, and credit card transactions.

Andrew Tobias' Managing Your Money. The most comprehensive financial planning program with checkbook and portfolio management, a calendar to-do list, and a tax planner. Calculates mortgage payments, whether to buy or lease a car or home.

Investing

Smart Investor. Published by "Money" Magazine, this is an on-line investing service, requiring a phone line and modem. Research on stocks, bonds, mutual funds, CDs and money market funds.

Taxes

Andrew Tobias' TaxCut. Question and answer format helps you determine which of more than 85 IRS tax forms to use. Keeps track of receipts and tax info all year 'round.

Turbotax. Has as many tax forms as Tobias' program plus more worksheets. Easy to read and use.